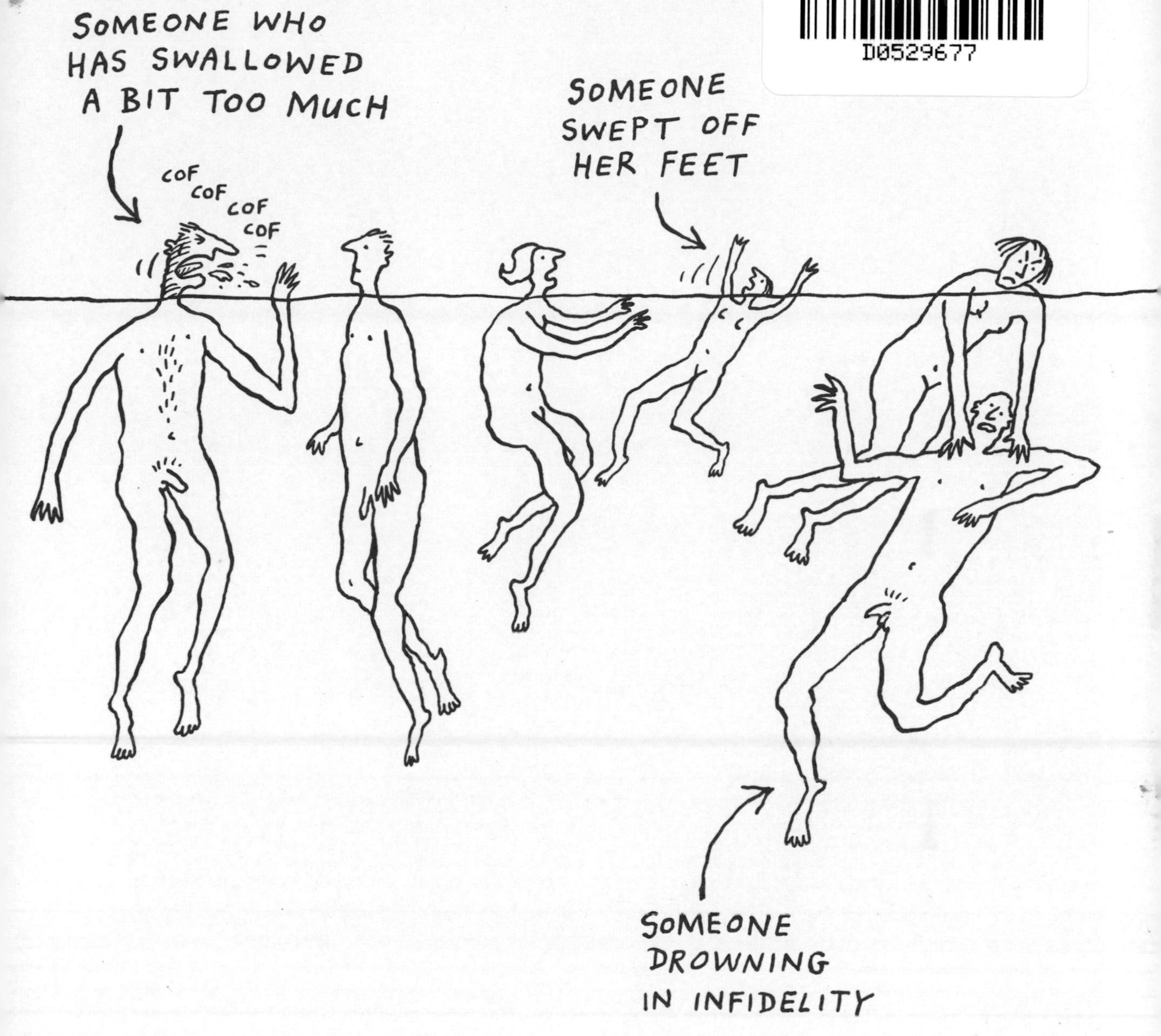
SOMEONE WHO HAS SWALLOWED A BIT TOO MUCH
COF COF COF COF
SOMEONE SWEPT OFF HER FEET
SOMEONE DROWNING IN INFIDELITY

THIS BOOK IS A GIFT TO:

_ _ _ _ _ _ _ _ _ _

WITH LOTS OF LOVE* FROM

_ _ _ _ _ _ _ _ _ _

* Read this book before jumping to any conclusions.

THE TRUTH ABOUT

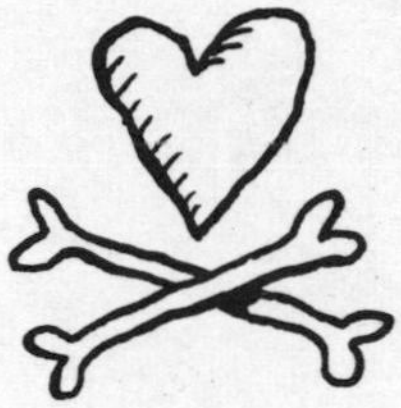

LOVE

MAKING LOVE —

SPURT

THE TRUTH ABOUT LOVE

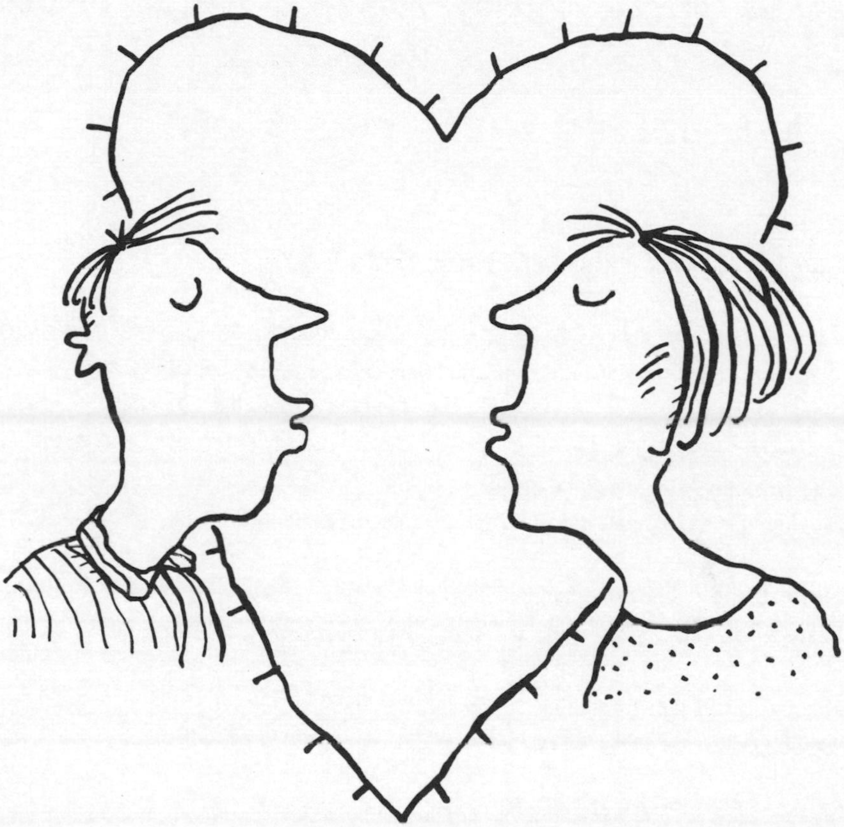

Steven Appleby

PLEASE NOTE –
Due to an error by the artist on page 62, 'LOVE' should read 'HATE' throughout.

SERIAL NUMBER: SA/99 Mk 1

ALL MY LOVE TO:

Jon Barraclough, Karen Brown, Liz Calder, Kasper de Graaf, Cathy Huszar, Linda McCarthy, Nicola Sherring, and Valentina

WHO ALL HELPED WITH THIS BOOK

For information address
Bloomsbury Publishing, 175 Fifth Avenue, New York, N.Y. 10010

Published by Bloomsbury Publishing, New York and London
Distributed to the trade by St. Martin's Press

A CIP catalogue record for this book
is available from the Library of Congress

ISBN 1-58234-065-X

First U.S. Edition 1999
10 9 8 7 6 5 4 3 2 1

Printed in Great Britain by Bath Press

Love will light up every
part of your life, showing
you that up until then
you had lived in
darkness

Steven Appleby.

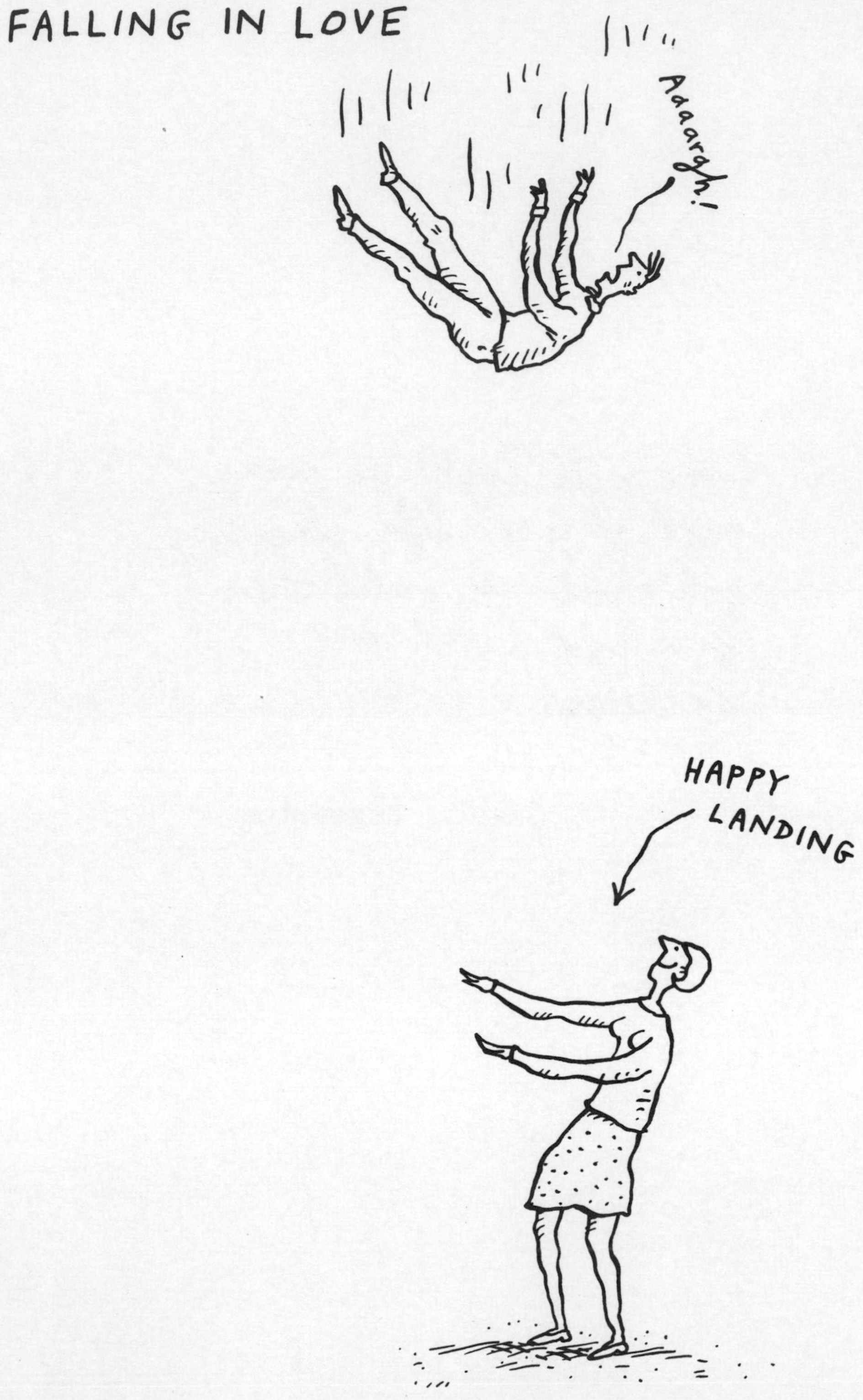
FALLING IN LOVE
Aaaargh!
HAPPY
LANDING

1

TRUE LOVE

Men and women, men and men and women and women. Love knows no boundaries and all combinations of sex, colour, race and creed fall in love with each other causing all sorts of happiness, joy, heartbreak and sadness. It happens all the time.

BRIAN
ROBERT
VERA
SANDY
BONSA

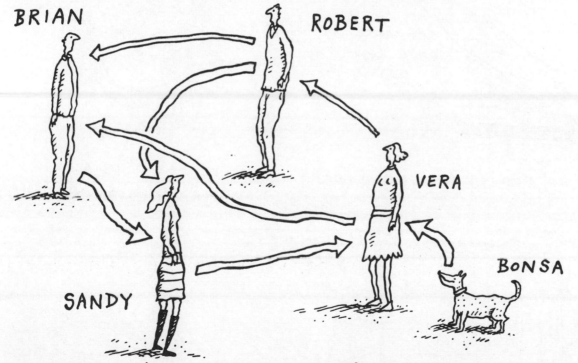

But before looking at its effects, perhaps we should understand exactly <u>WHAT</u> love is...

HERE ARE SOME CURRENT THEORIES concerning the NATURE OF LOVE:

i – LOVE IS A DISEASE.

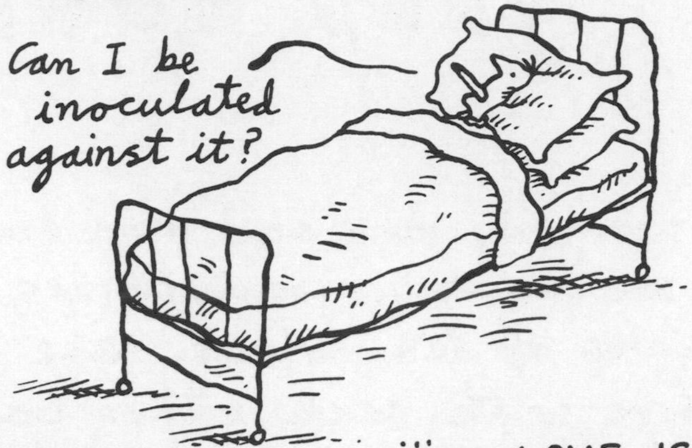
Can I be inoculated against it?

ii – LOVE IS AN ALIEN GERM WARFARE ATTACK.

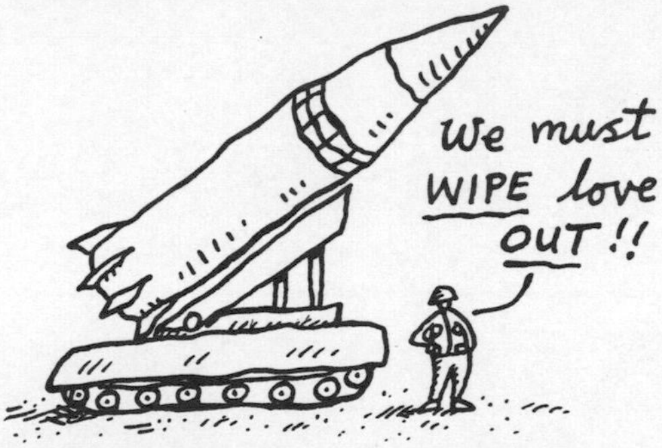
We must WIPE love OUT!!

iii – LOVE IS A CHEMICAL REACTION.

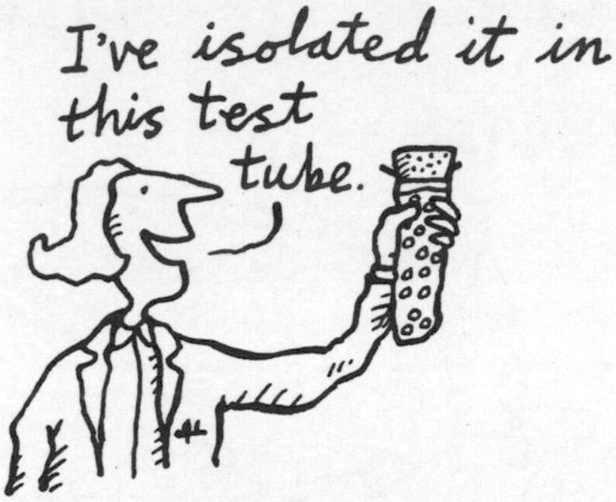
I've isolated it in this test tube.

iv – LOVE IS AN ILLUSION.

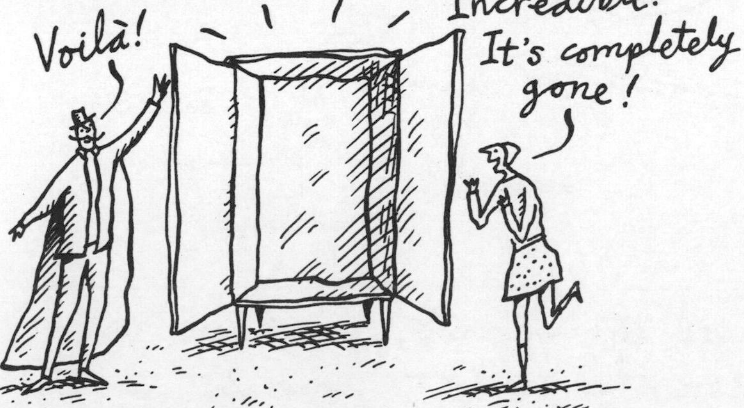
Voilà!
Incredible! It's completely gone!

v – LOVE IS A SPIRITUAL EXPERIENCE.

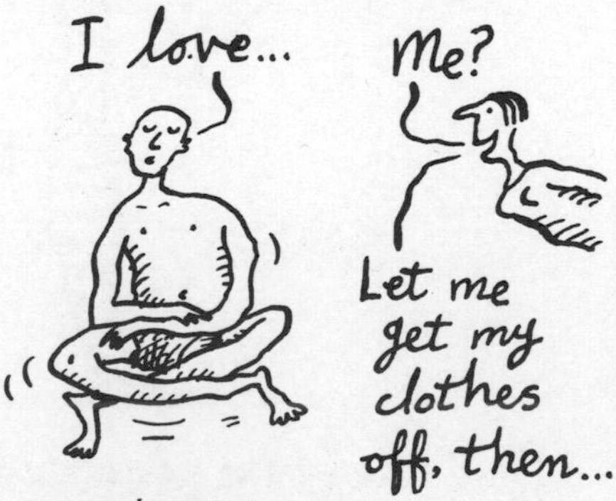
I love...
Me?
Let me get my clothes off, then...

Some scientists, who managed to synthesise love in a laboratory, injected it into rats then sent them into space in a rocket. The rats composed banal love poetry, wrote a few rather second-rate pop songs and then died in a mutual suicide pact. The experiment was not regarded as a success and was never repeated.

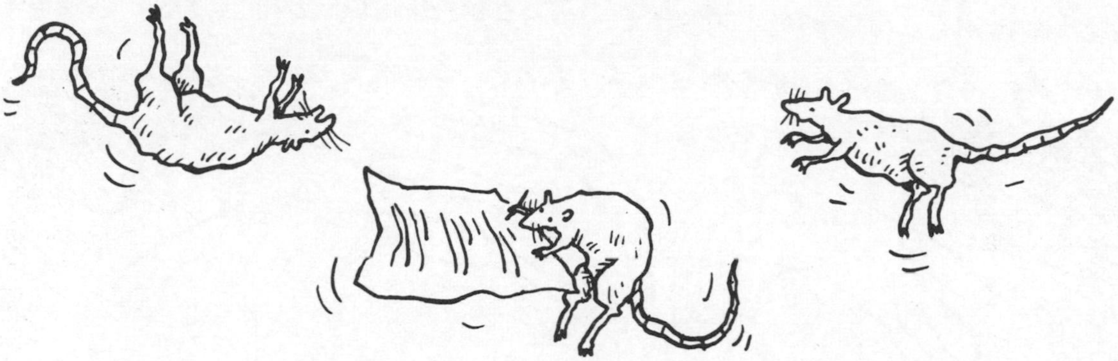

It is possible to buy 'tabs' of love on the black market, but it is highly addictive and the resulting emotion extremely dangerous and uncontrollable. The government are in the process of banning love on the advice of the very scientists who created it. All stocks will be destroyed and the experimental establishment sealed up for a hundred years.

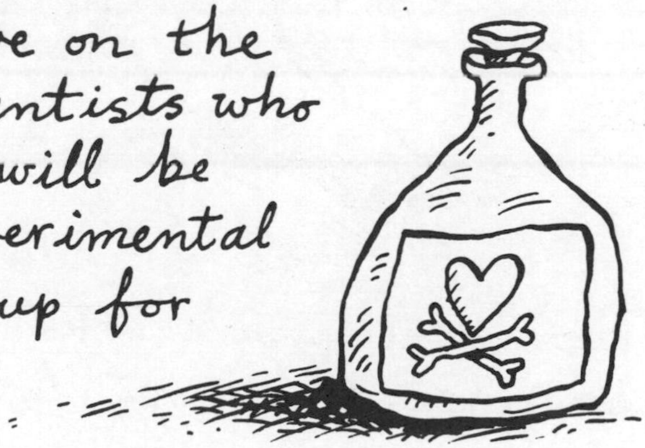

WHERE **LOVE** COMES FROM

However, all this government research is interesting but misleading. In fact, LOVE is a naturally occurring phenomenon. This rare picture shows LOVE erupting, as it has done throughout history, from a geyser in an obscure mountain range somewhere in Iceland. From here it spreads on the trade winds to all parts of the earth.

The local people who live near this geyser are amongst the most lovesick in the world.

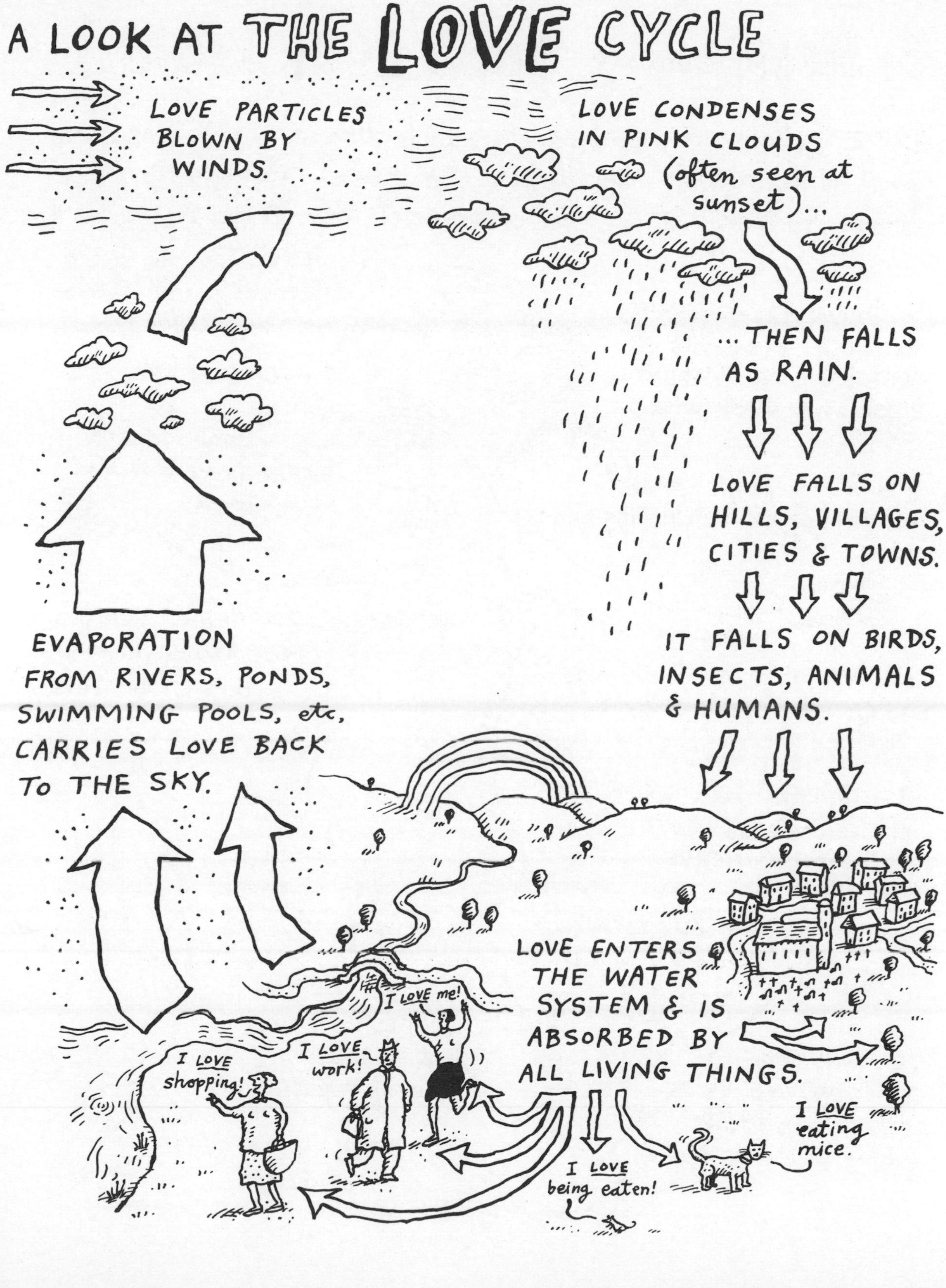
A LOOK AT THE LOVE CYCLE
LOVE PARTICLES BLOWN BY WINDS.
LOVE CONDENSES IN PINK CLOUDS (often seen at sunset)...
...THEN FALLS AS RAIN.
LOVE FALLS ON HILLS, VILLAGES, CITIES & TOWNS.
IT FALLS ON BIRDS, INSECTS, ANIMALS & HUMANS.
LOVE ENTERS THE WATER SYSTEM & IS ABSORBED BY ALL LIVING THINGS.
I LOVE me!
I LOVE work!
I LOVE shopping!
I LOVE eating mice.
I LOVE being eaten!
EVAPORATION FROM RIVERS, PONDS, SWIMMING POOLS, etc, CARRIES LOVE BACK TO THE SKY.

So HOW, exactly, DOES LOVE WORK?

LOVE enters our bodies through the air we breathe and the water we drink. It then travels to the brain where it sets a chemical reaction in motion.

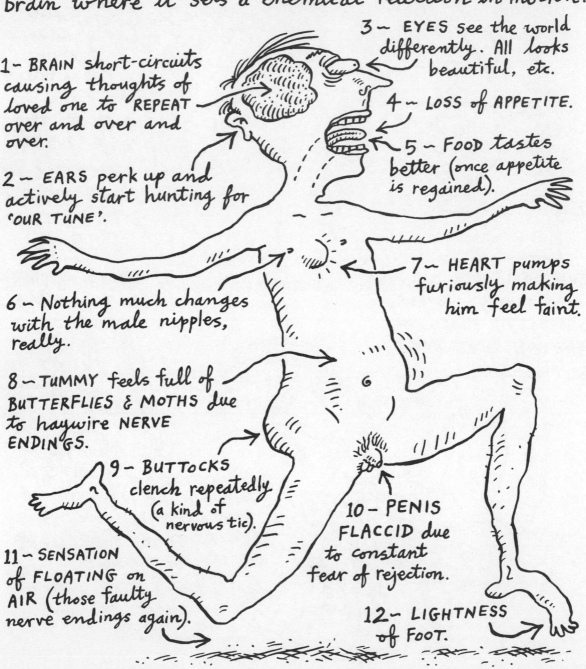

1 - BRAIN short-circuits causing thoughts of loved one to 'REPEAT' over and over and over.

2 ~ EARS perk up and actively start hunting for 'OUR TUNE'.

3 ~ EYES see the world differently. All looks beautiful, etc.

4 ~ LOSS of APPETITE.

5 ~ FOOD tastes better (once appetite is regained).

6 ~ Nothing much changes with the male nipples, really.

7 ~ HEART pumps furiously making him feel faint.

8 ~ TUMMY feels full of BUTTERFLIES & MOTHS due to haywire NERVE ENDINGS.

9 - BUTTOCKS clench repeatedly (a kind of nervous tic).

10 - PENIS FLACCID due to constant fear of rejection.

11 - SENSATION of FLOATING on AIR (those faulty nerve endings again).

12 - LIGHTNESS of FOOT.

This chemical reaction triggers the eyes to seek out a 'loved one', whereupon the brain short-circuits and sends tiny messages down the nerves to most parts of the body causing them to go haywire.

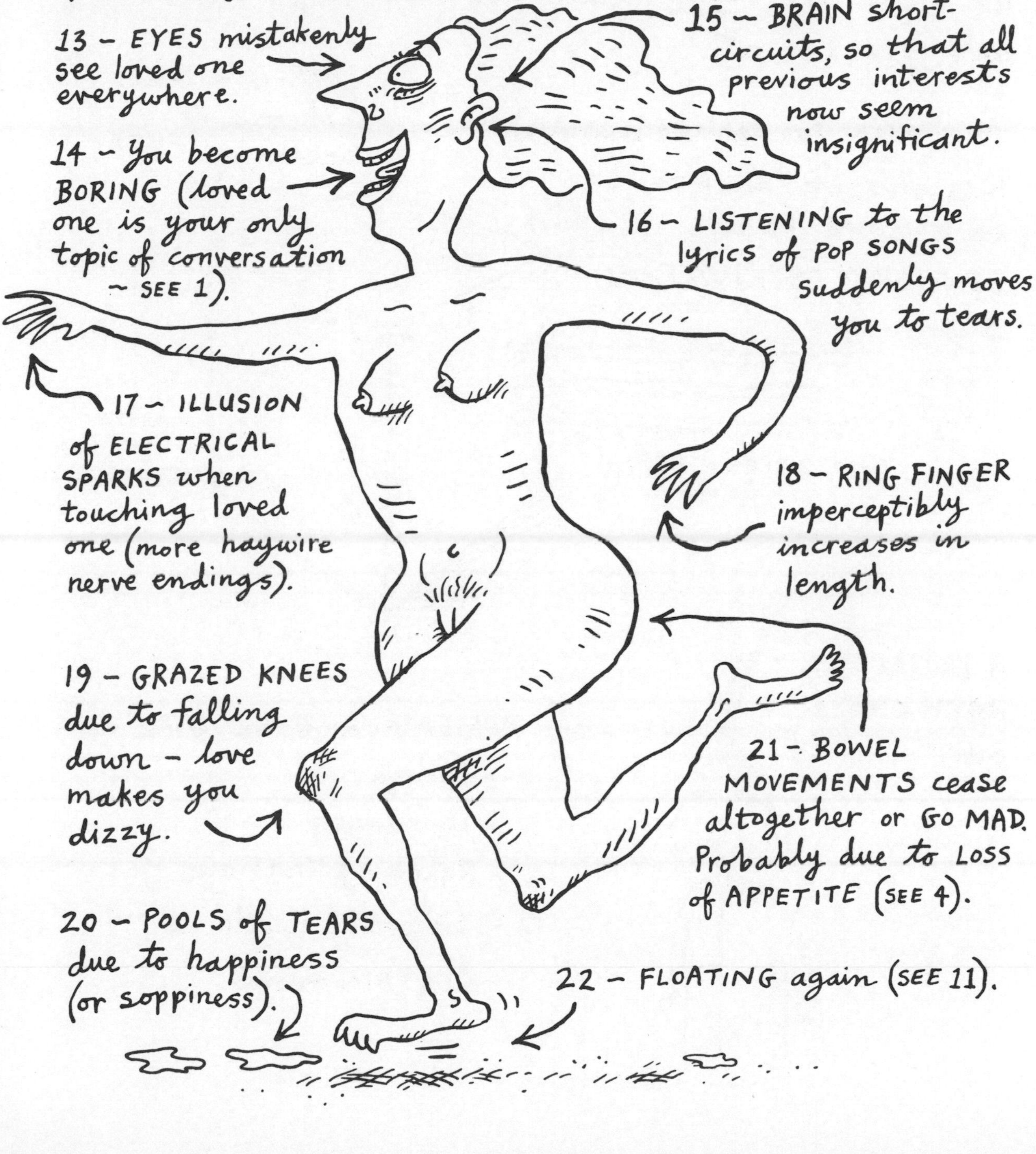
13 - EYES mistakenly see loved one everywhere.
14 - You become BORING (loved one is your only topic of conversation - SEE 1).
15 - BRAIN short-circuits, so that all previous interests now seem insignificant.
16 - LISTENING to the lyrics of POP SONGS suddenly moves you to tears.
17 - ILLUSION of ELECTRICAL SPARKS when touching loved one (more haywire nerve endings).
18 - RING FINGER imperceptibly increases in length.
19 - GRAZED KNEES due to falling down - love makes you dizzy.
20 - POOLS of TEARS due to happiness (or soppiness).
21 - BOWEL MOVEMENTS cease altogether or GO MAD. Probably due to LOSS of APPETITE (SEE 4).
22 - FLOATING again (SEE 11).

FIGHTING IT!

SOME PEOPLE, of course, don't want to FALL IN LOVE **AT ALL!** Here are some suggestions to help you resist.

THIS MAN (or perhaps WOMAN) has chosen to live in a LOVE-FREE SENSORY DEPRIVATION BOX:

LOVE is a TRAP! I choose to remain FREE!

AIR HOLES

WASTE OUT →

FOOD, WATER & HEAT GO IN

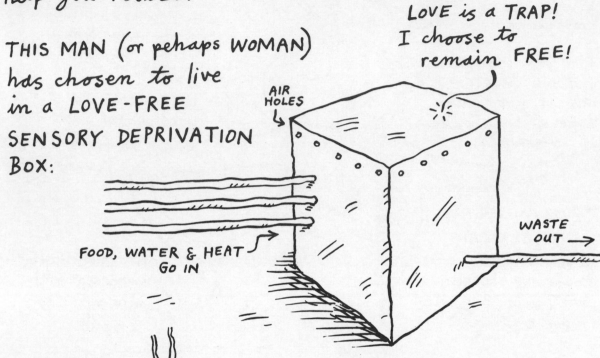

A PROTECTIVE ANTI-LOVE SUIT:

REMEMBER to be WARY OF:
- Spring.
- Hormones.
- Reaching THAT age.
- Inherited neediness.
- CERTAIN foods.

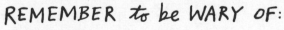

SOME *familiar* LOVE SUBSTITUTES...

CATS (lots of them):

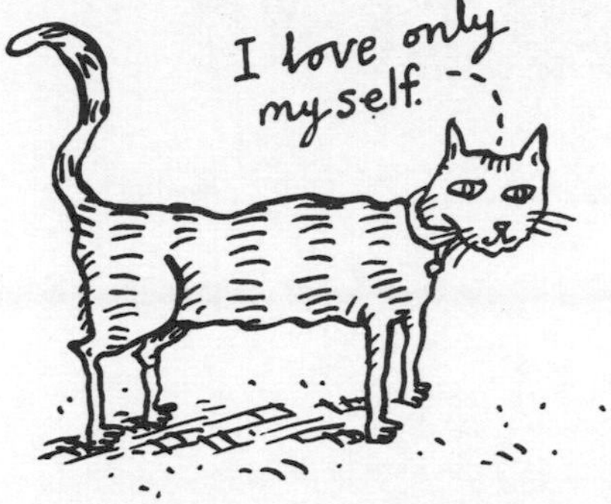

I love only myself.

ROMANTIC NOVELS:

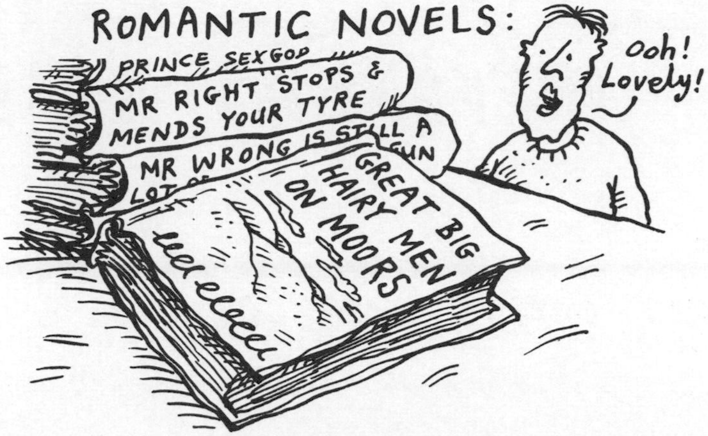

PRINCE SEXGOD
MR RIGHT STOPS & MENDS YOUR TYRE
MR WRONG IS STILL A
GREAT BIG HAIRY MEN ON MOORS
Ooh! Lovely!

EATING:

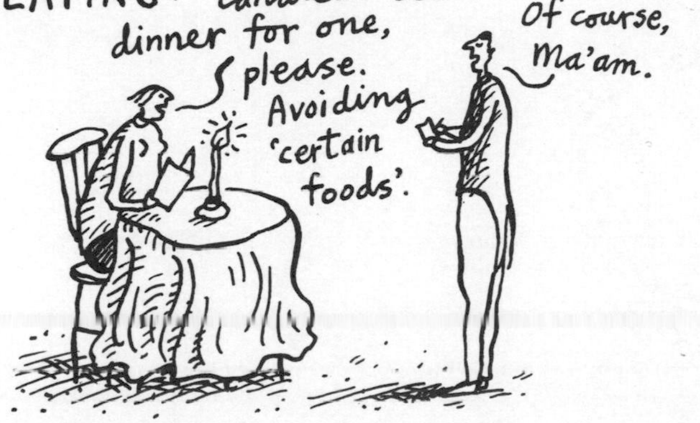

Candlelit set dinner for one, please. Avoiding 'certain foods'.
Of course, Ma'am.

PROSTITUTES:

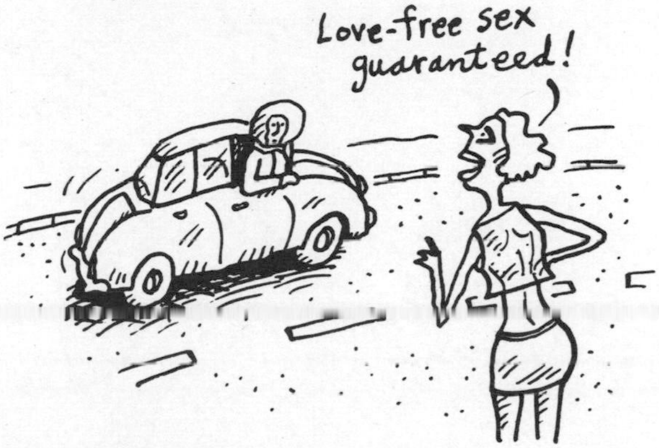

Love-free sex guaranteed!

GARDENING:

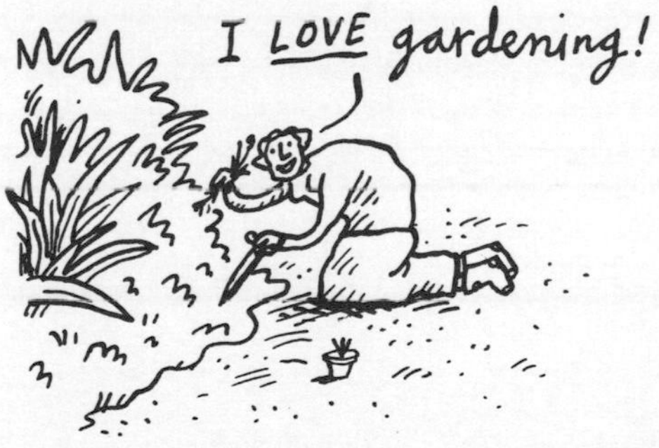

I LOVE gardening!

SEEING FILMS:

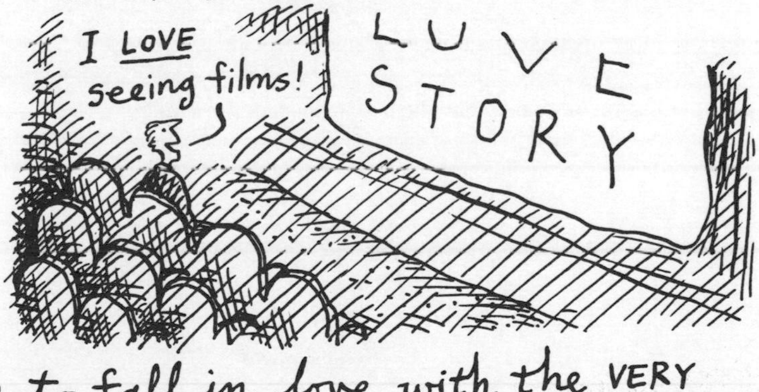

I LOVE seeing films!
LOVE STORY

It is, however, possible to fall in love with the VERY ACTIVITIES intended to DISTRACT you from love – a fact which catches many people unawares.

2

Perhaps it's time we took a look at the many

DIFFERENT KINDS OF LOVE

ALL-CONSUMING LOVE

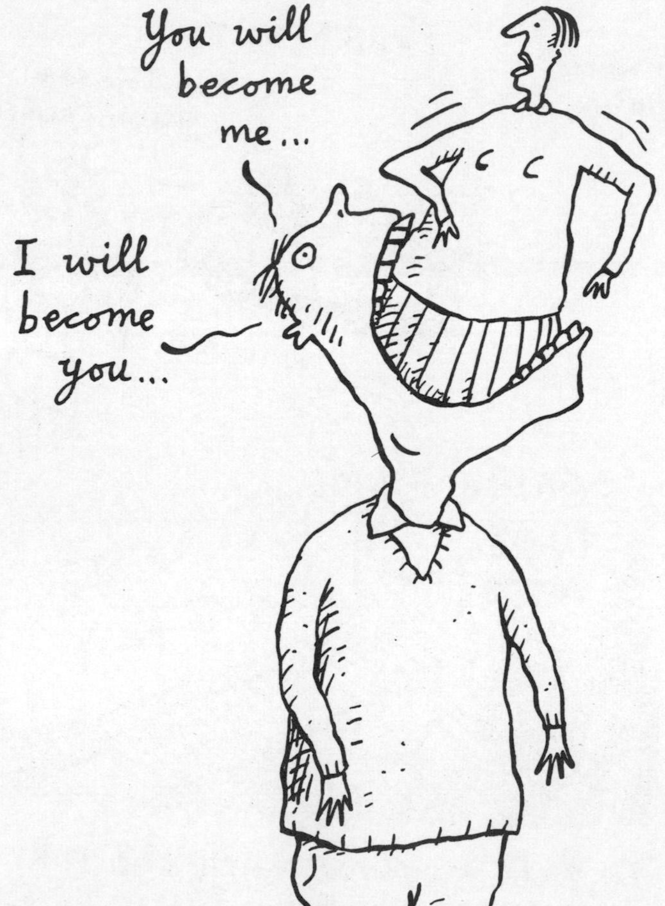
You will become me...
I will become you...

OBSESSIVE LOVE

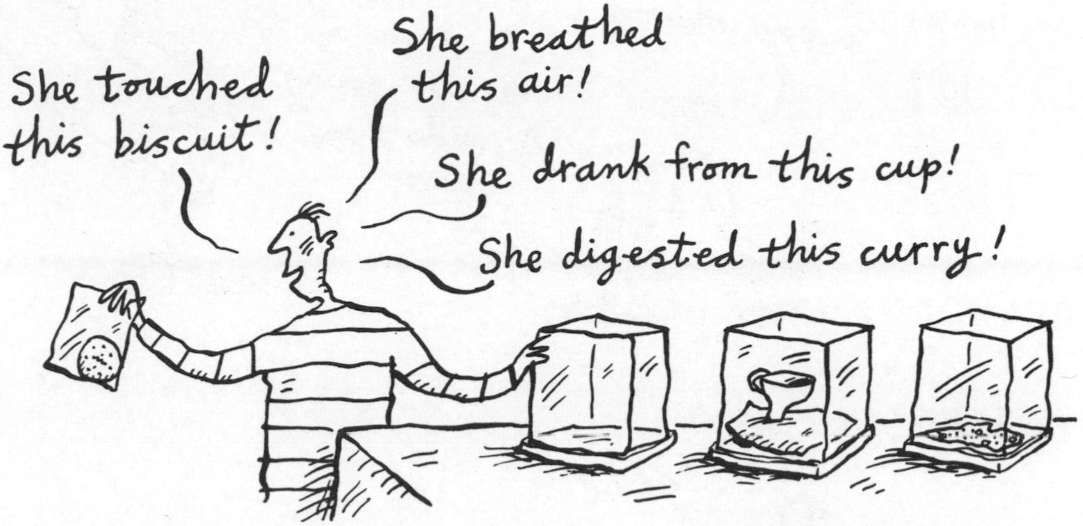
She touched this biscuit!
She breathed this air!
She drank from this cup!
She digested this curry!

SPIRITUAL LOVE

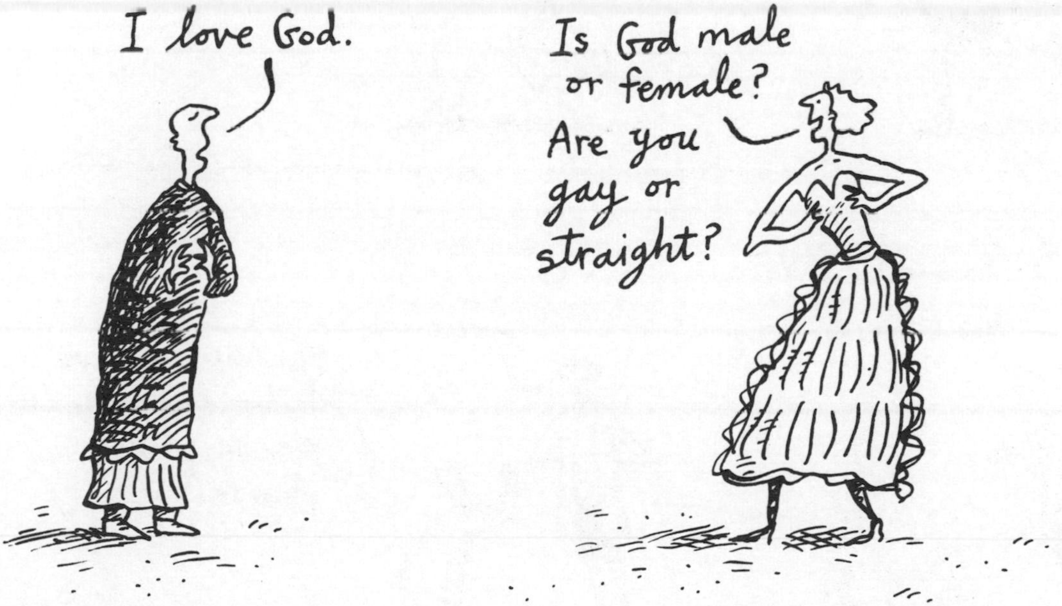
I love God.
Is God male or female? Are you gay or straight?

PUPPY LOVE

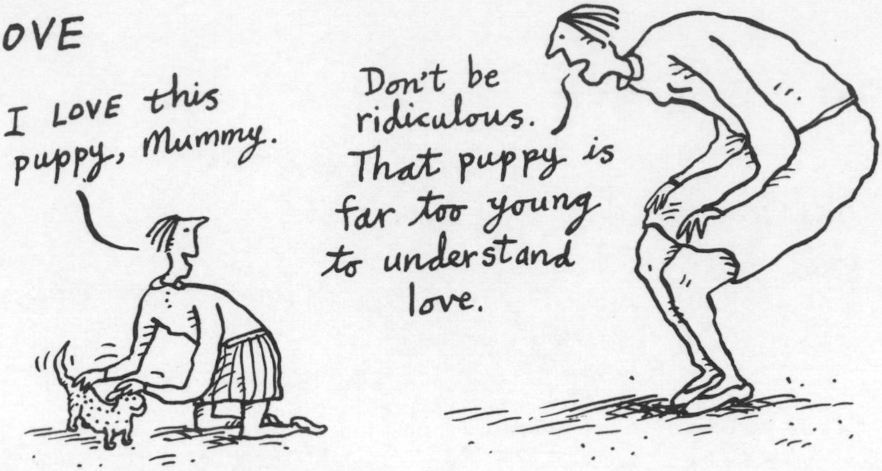
I LOVE this puppy, Mummy.
Don't be ridiculous. That puppy is far too young to understand love.

POSSESSIVE LOVE

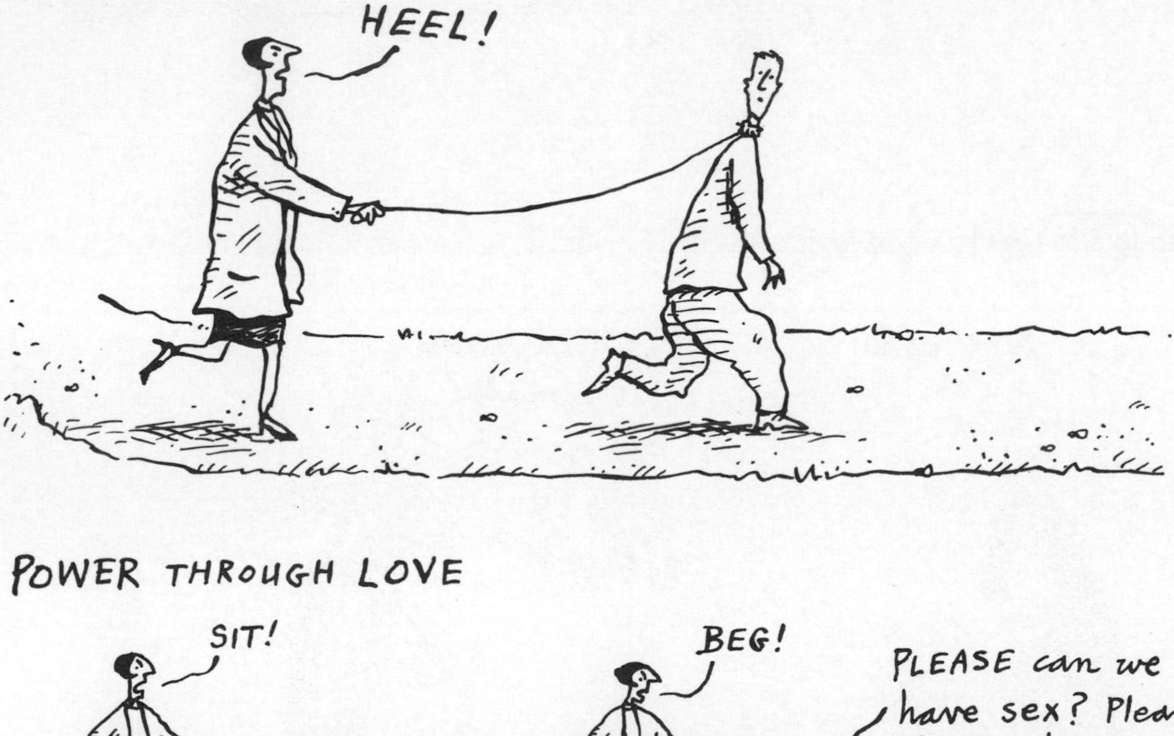
HEEL!

POWER THROUGH LOVE

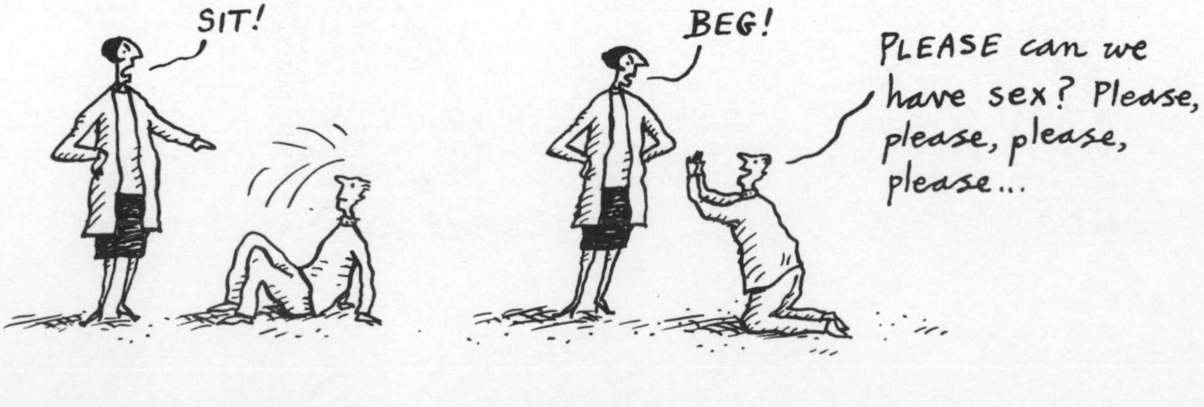
SIT!
BEG!
PLEASE can we have sex? Please, please, please, please...

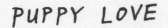

CUPBOARD LOVE

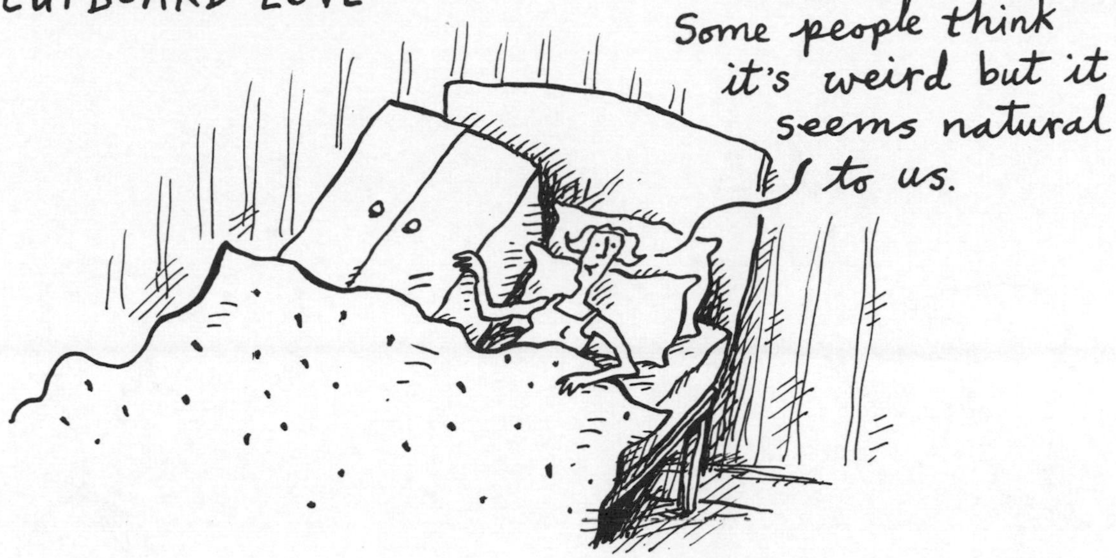
Some people think it's weird but it seems natural to us.

MOMENTARY ORGASMIC LOVE

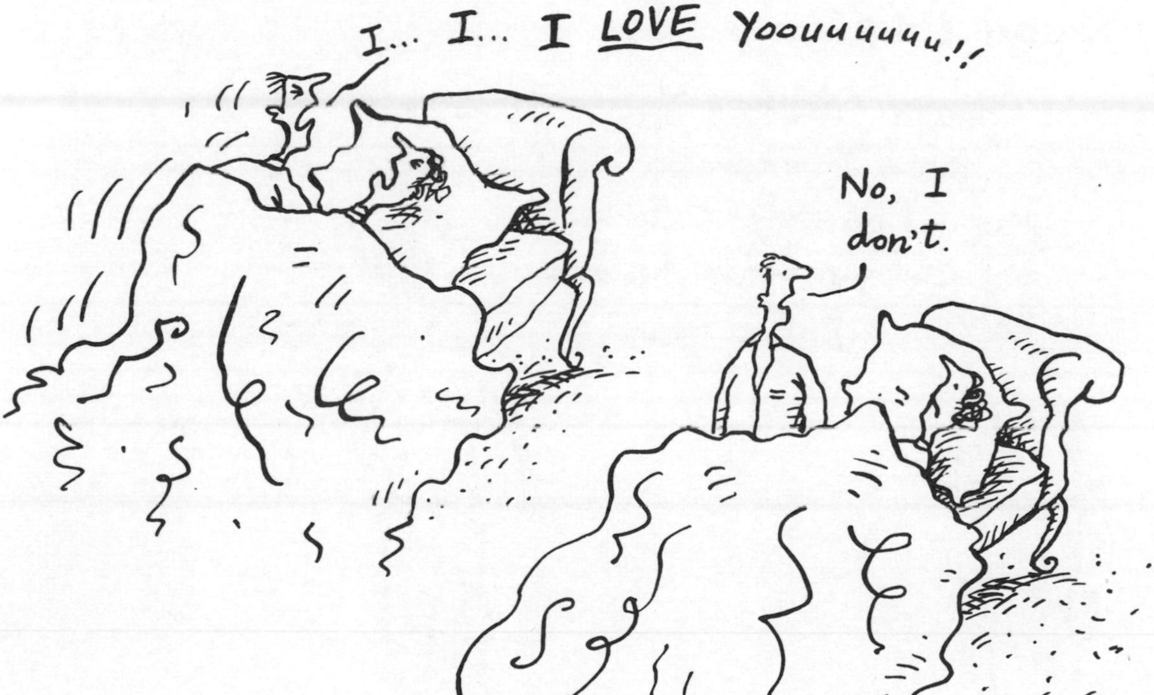
I... I... I LOVE Yoouuuuuu!!
No, I don't.

REPRESSED LOVE

Dad, I...
I... I...

Son, I...
I... I...

TOUGH LOVE

You're flabby. You
need to exercise.
I'm only telling
you this because
I love you.

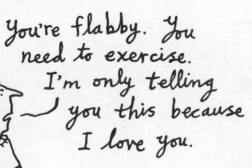

PLATONIC LOVE

where's the fun in THAT?

UNREQUITED LOVE

He's there again, Ma'am.
YAWN...

LOVE OF SHOES

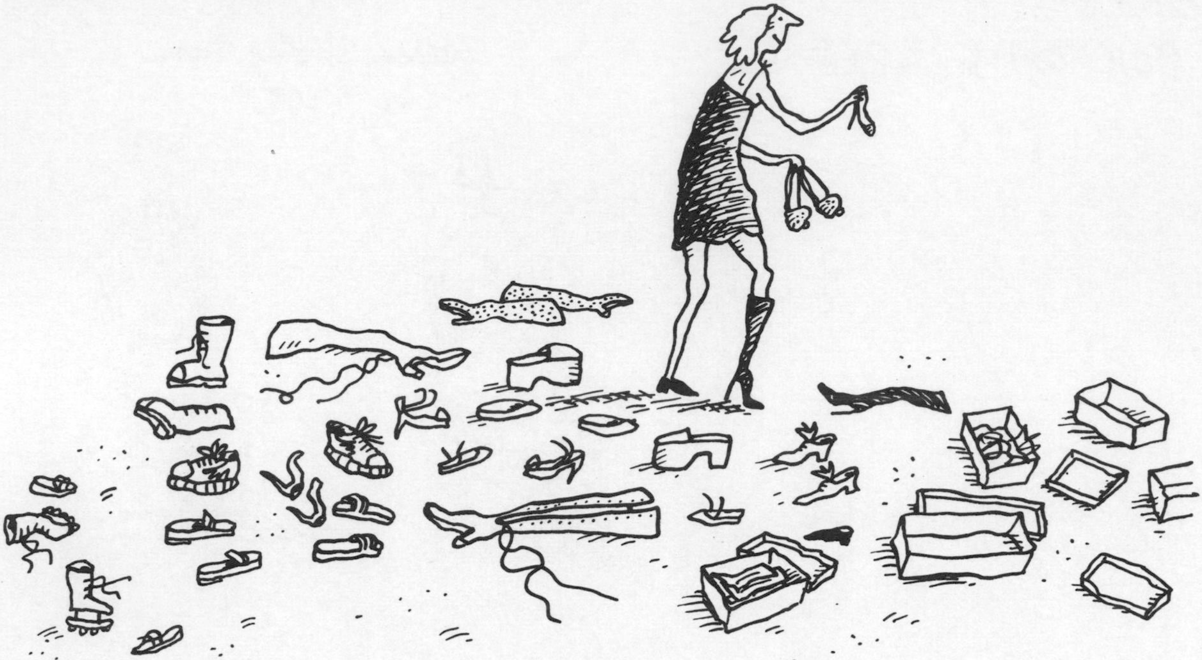

LOVE OF YOUR CAR

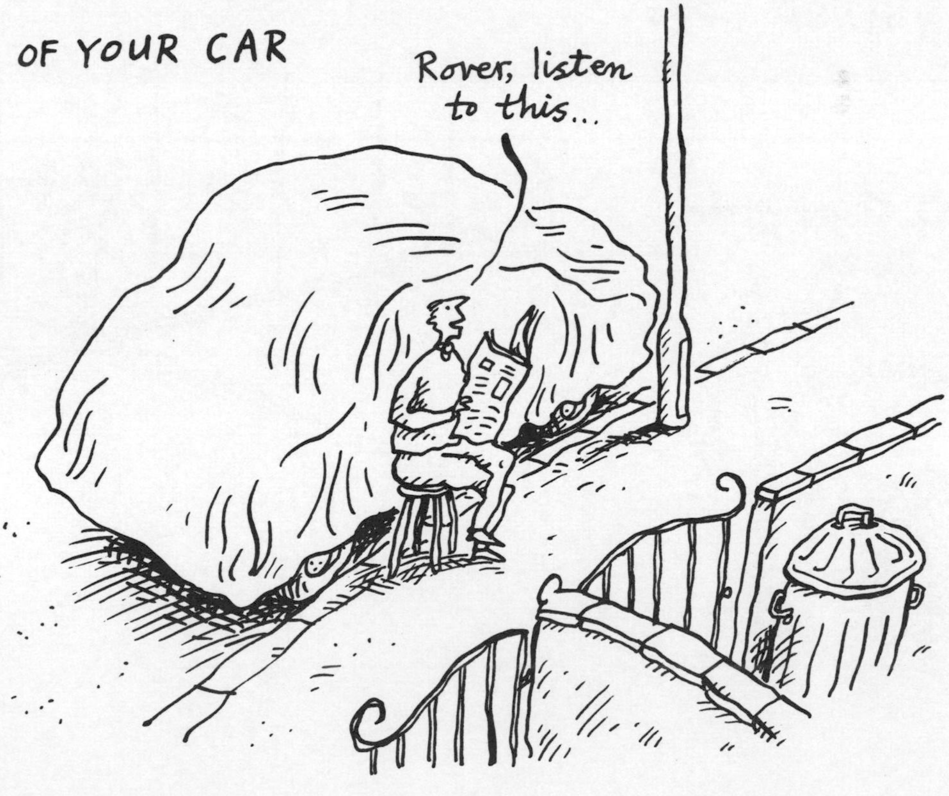
Rover, listen to this...

SQUEAMISH LOVE

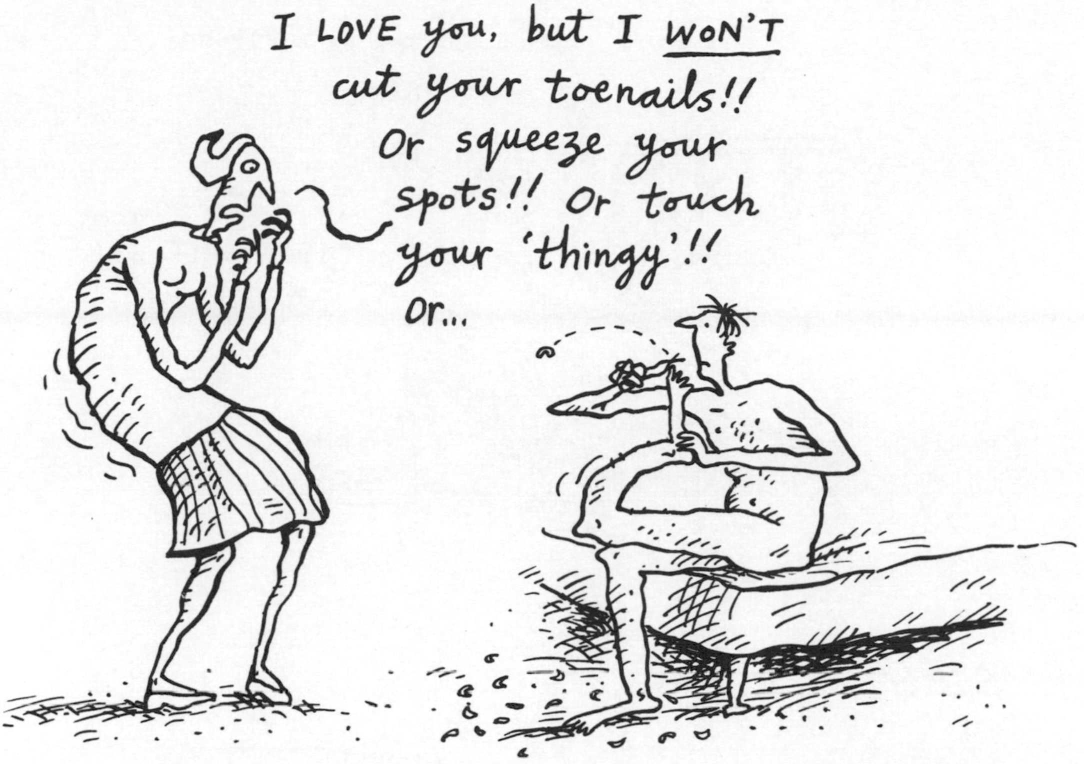
I LOVE you, but I WON'T cut your toenails!! Or squeeze your spots!! Or touch your 'thingy'!! Or...

KINKY LOVE

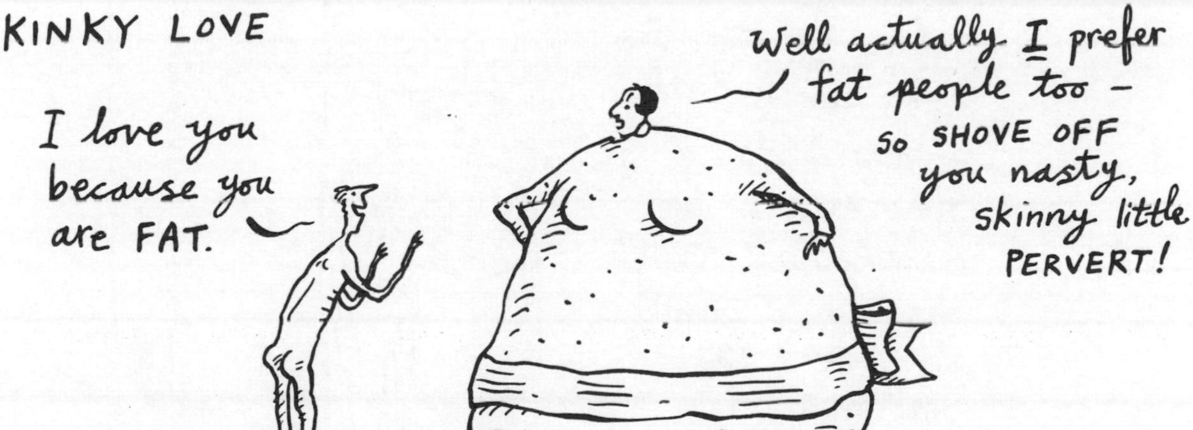
I love you because you are FAT.
Well actually I prefer fat people too – so SHOVE OFF you nasty, skinny little PERVERT!

JEALOUS LOVE

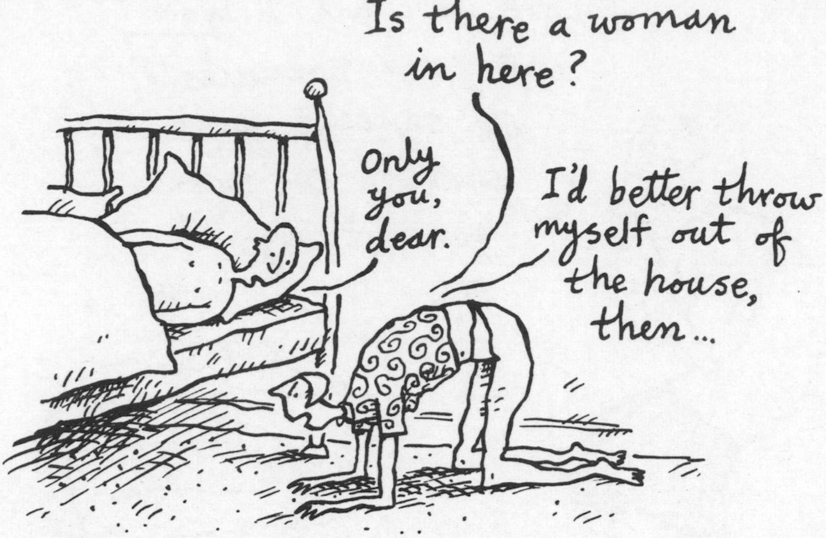
Is there a woman in here?
Only you, dear.
I'd better throw myself out of the house, then...

NARCISSISTIC LOVE

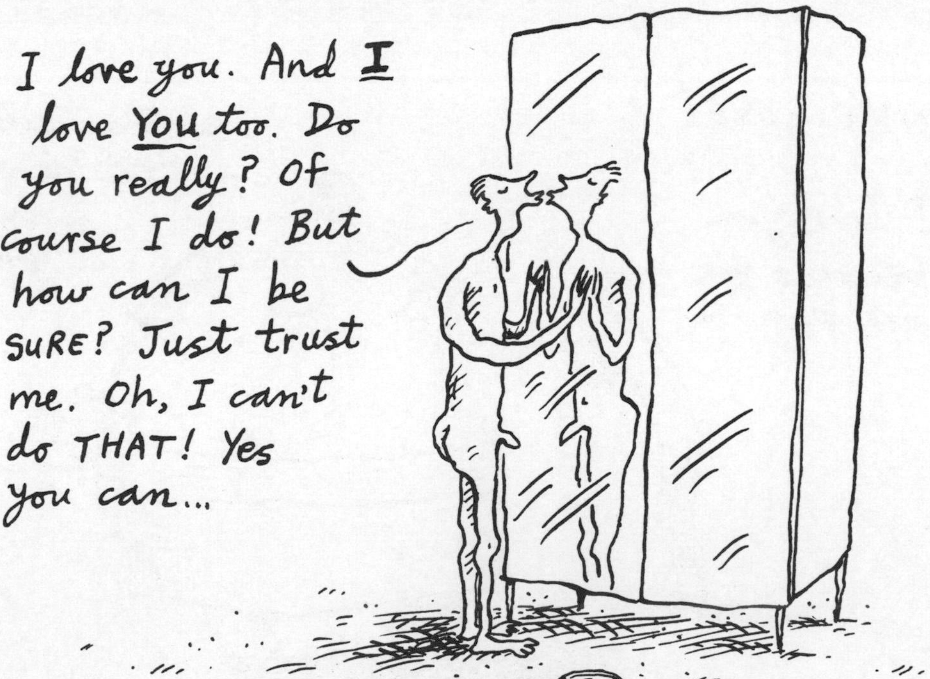
I love you. And I love YOU too. Do you really? Of course I do! But how can I be SURE? Just trust me. Oh, I can't do THAT! Yes you can...

CUDDLY & TOUCHY LOVE

SURGICALLY JOINED TOGETHER.

HAPPY EVER AFTER LOVE

creak creak creak creak creak...

LOVE OF T.V.

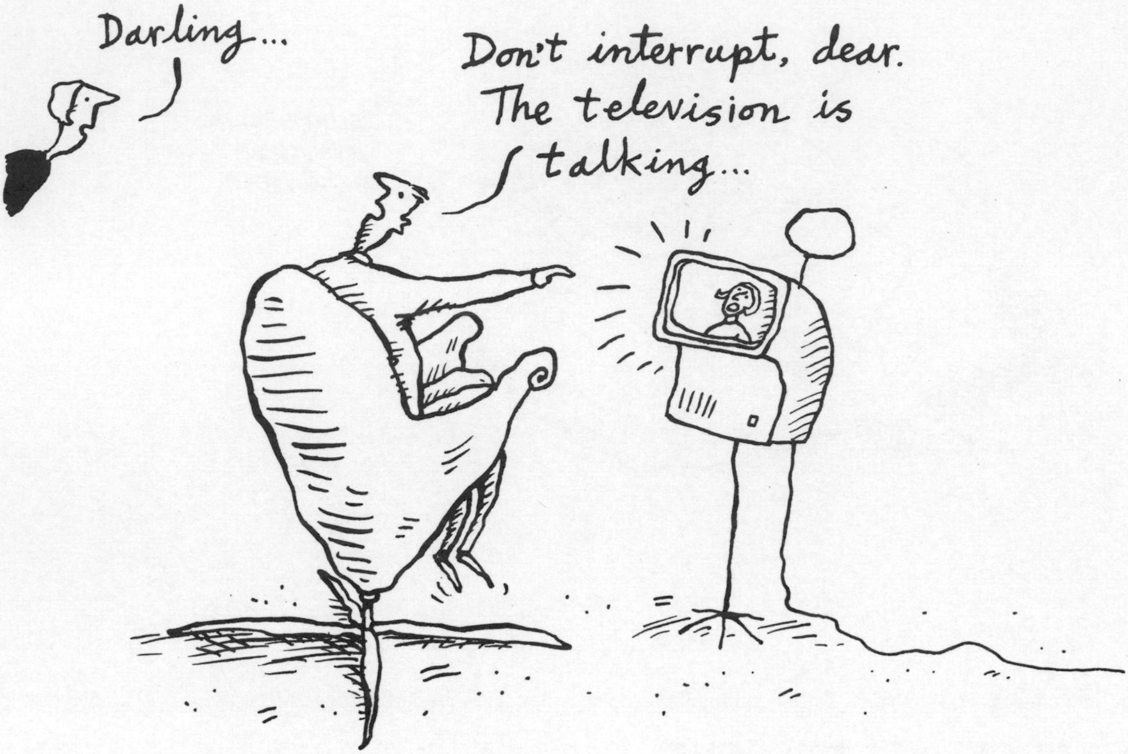
Darling...
Don't interrupt, dear. The television is talking...

DOGGY LOVE

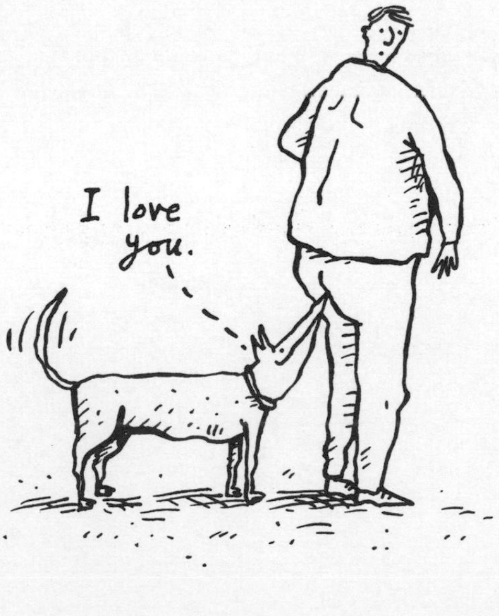
I love you.

LOVE OF COFFEE

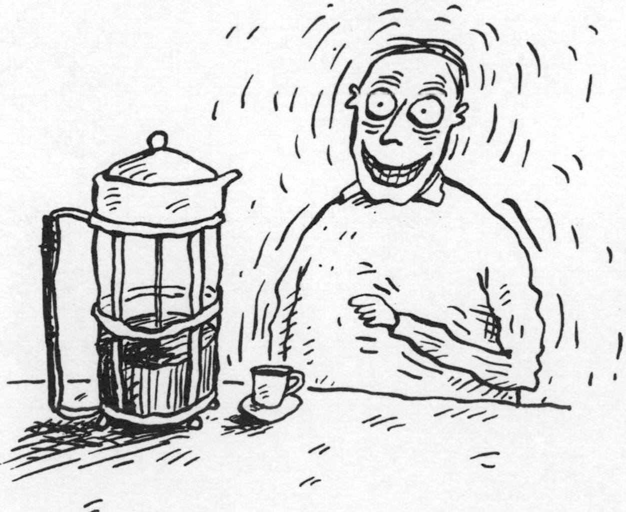

NEEDY LOVE

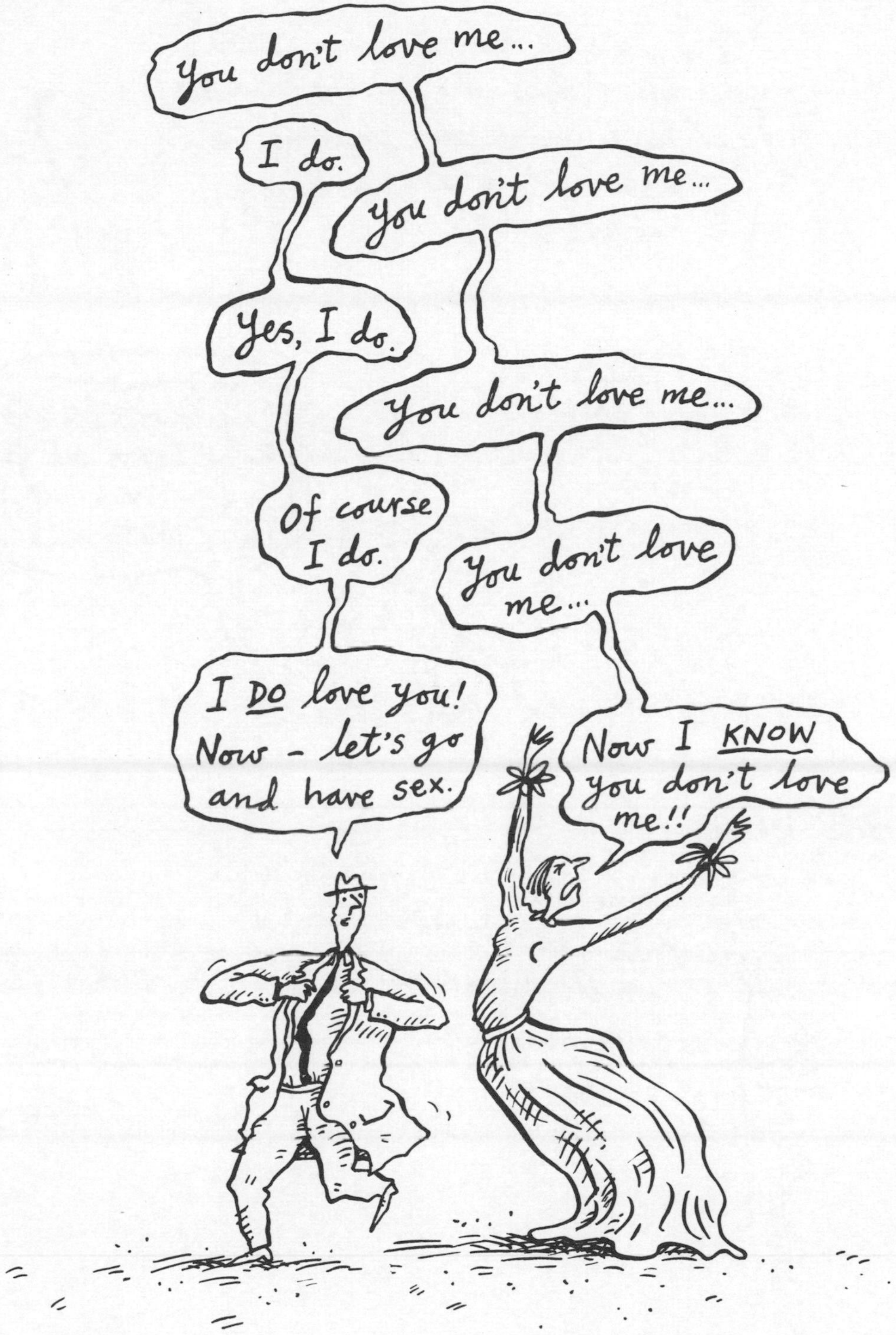
You don't love me...
I do.
You don't love me...
Yes, I do.
You don't love me...
Of course I do.
You don't love me...
I DO love you! Now - let's go and have sex.
Now I KNOW you don't love me!!

CALCULATED LOVE

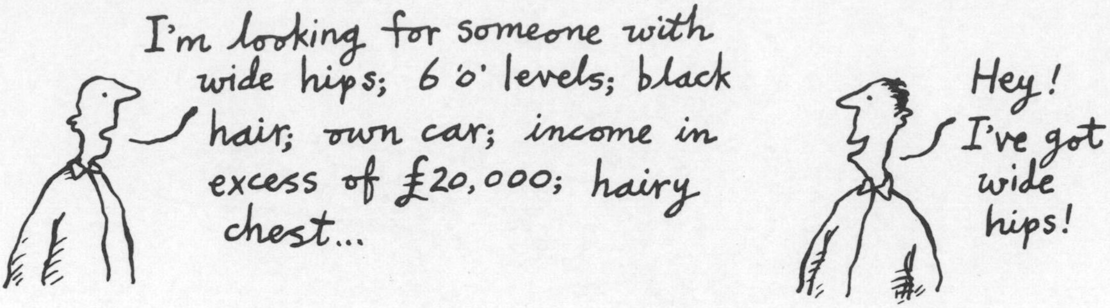
I'm looking for someone with wide hips; 6 'o' levels; black hair; own car; income in excess of £20,000; hairy chest...
Hey! I've got wide hips!

TEENAGE LOVE

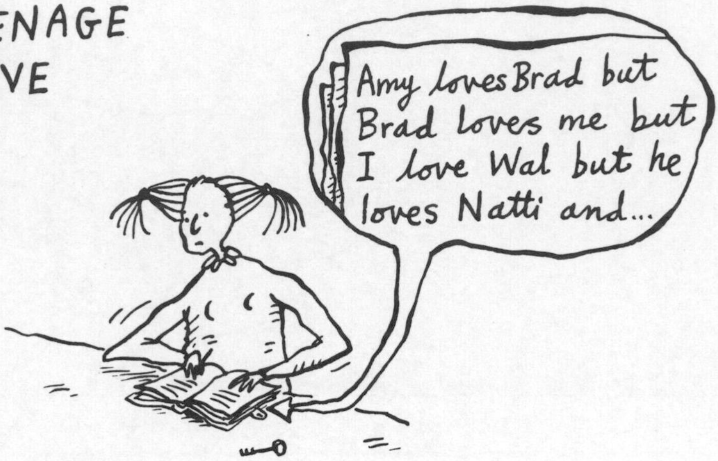
Amy loves Brad but Brad loves me but I love Wal but he loves Natti and...

NUDE LOVE

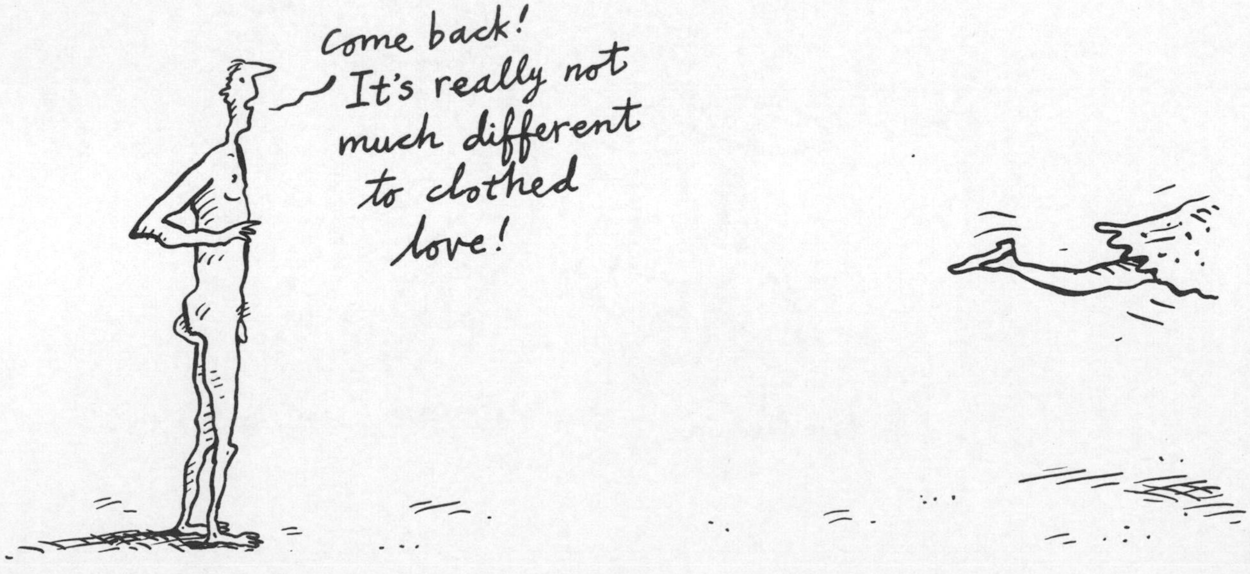
Come back! It's really not much different to clothed love!

LOVE OF YOUR CARDIGAN

That old thing? I threw it out.

LOVE OF YOUR COUNTRY

Kinky!

LOVE OF THE COUNTRYSIDE

squeak squeak squeak squeak...

GUILTY LOVE

STIFLING LOVE

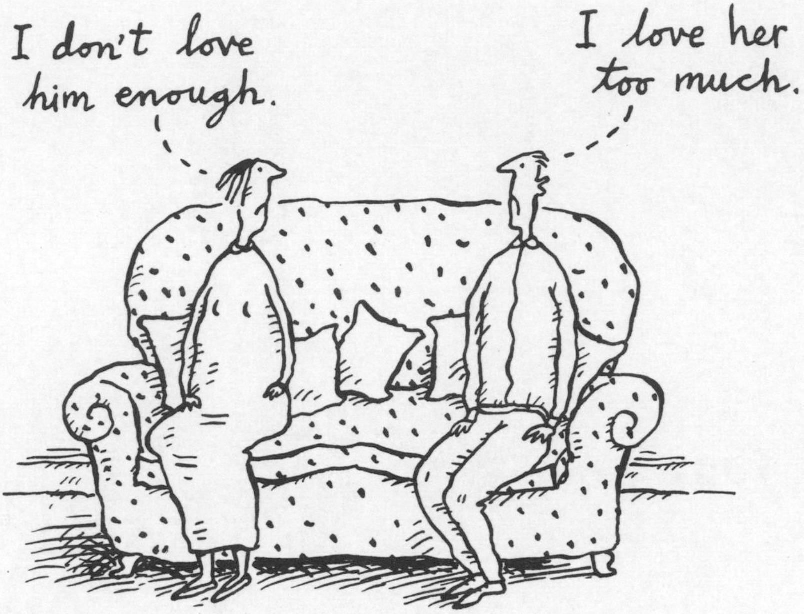
I don't love him enough.
I love her too much.

THE LOVE THAT DARE NOT SPEAK ITS NAME

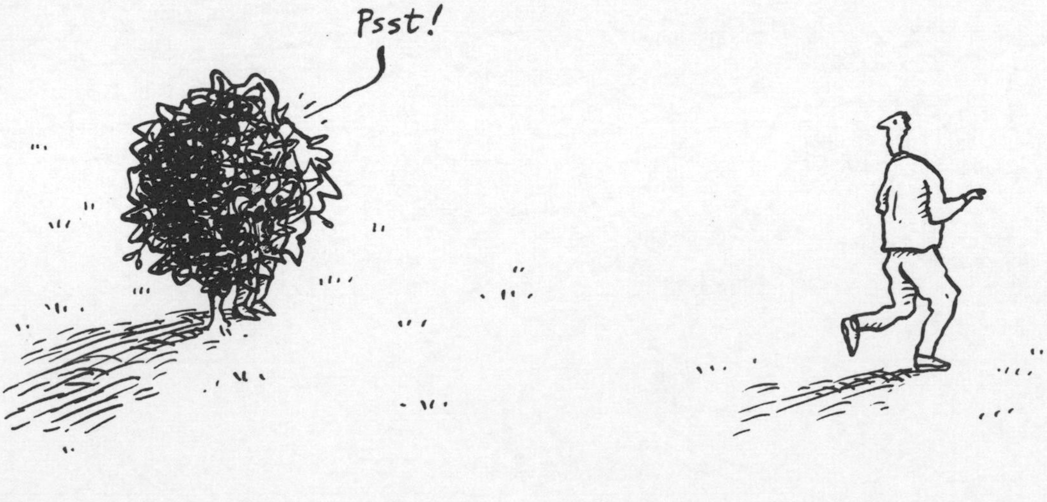
Psst!

UNCONDITIONAL LOVE

Mummy!

DAMAGING LOVE

I love your brother, but I don't love you.
I never have.
But I love you, Mummy.

LOVE FOR SMALL FURRY CREATURES

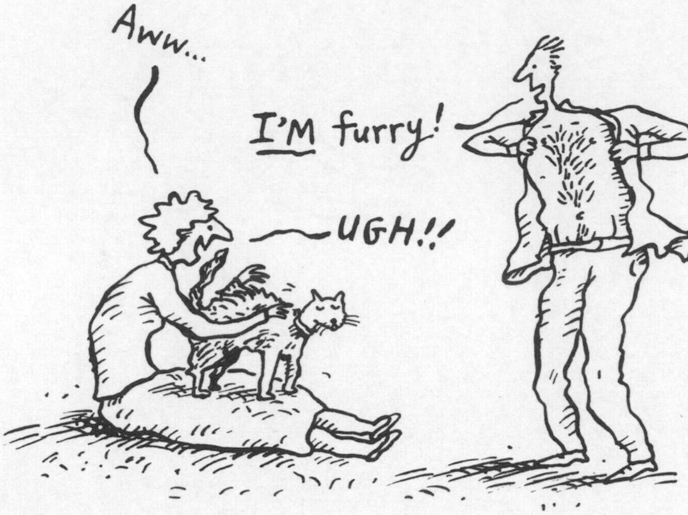
Aww...
I'M furry!
UGH!!

SWEET LOVE

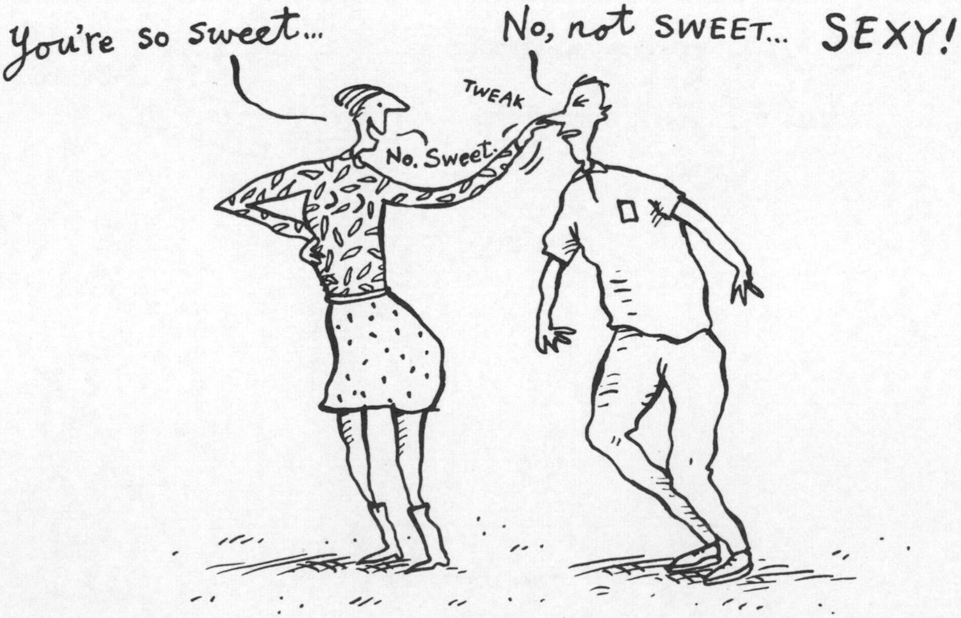
You're so sweet...
No, not SWEET... SEXY!
TWEAK
No. Sweet.

LOVE OF A GOOD BOOK

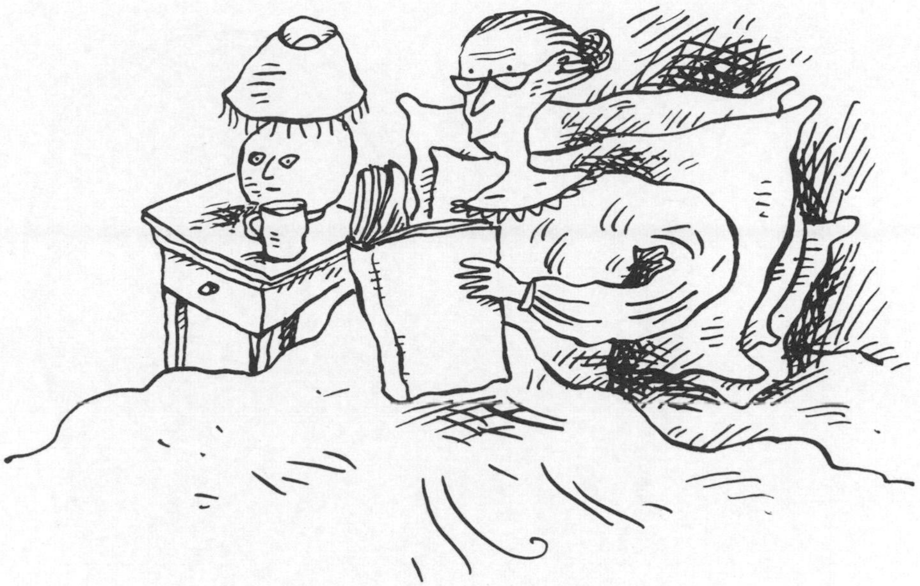

LOVE OF A CUP OF COCOA

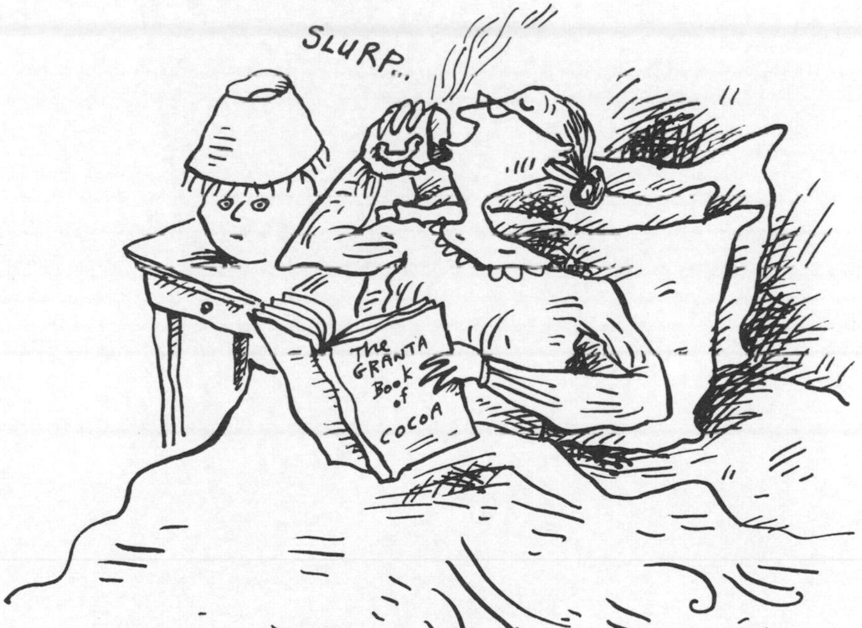
SLURP...
The GRANTA Book of COCOA

TRAGIC LOVE

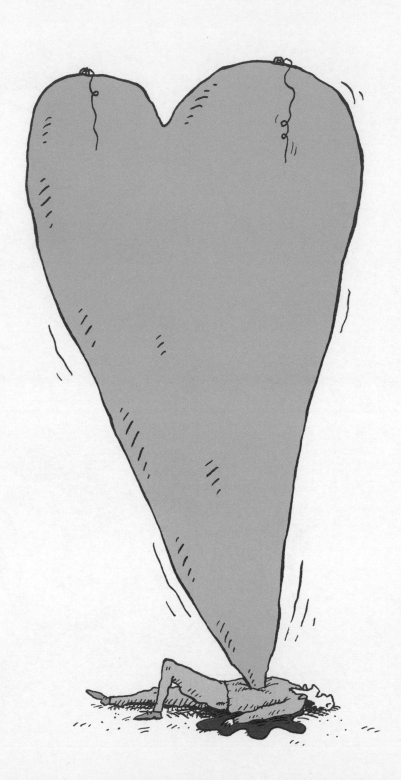

BLIND LOVE

Love makes you even blinder than masturbating. For example, a newly-in-love young lady can tolerate <u>ANYTHING!</u>

SNORING:

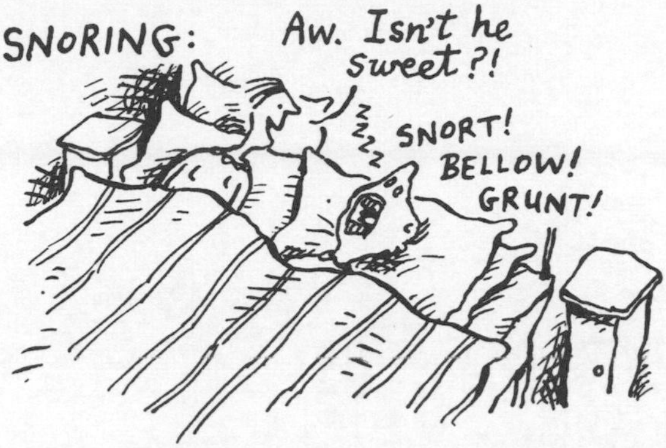
Aw. Isn't he sweet?!
ZZZZ
SNORT!
BELLOW!
GRUNT!

NOSE PICKING:

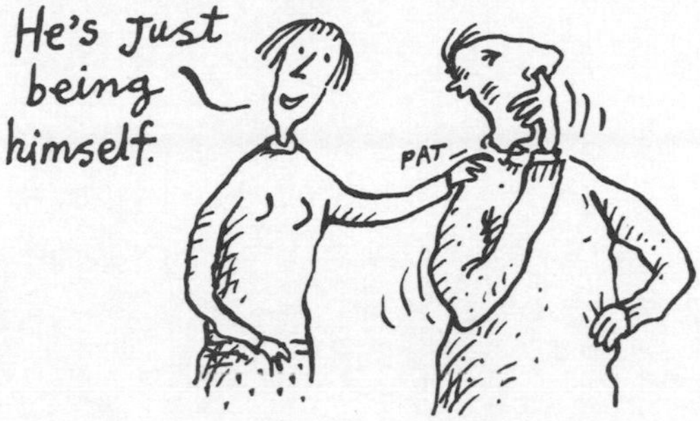
He's just being himself.
PAT

BUM SCRATCHING:

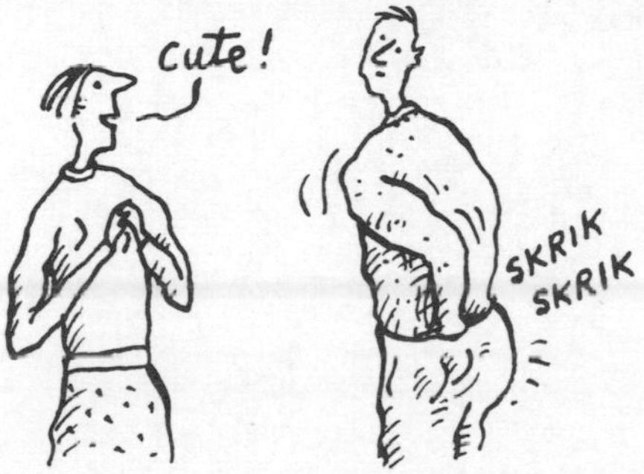
cute!
SKRIK
SKRIK

FARTING:

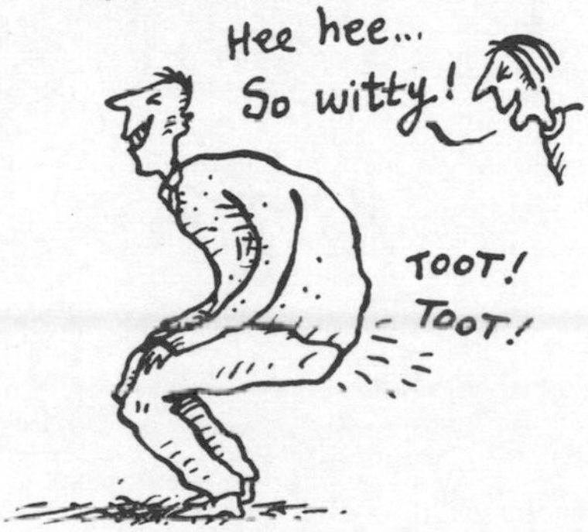
Hee hee... So witty!
TOOT!
TOOT!

STINKY FEET & ARMPITS:

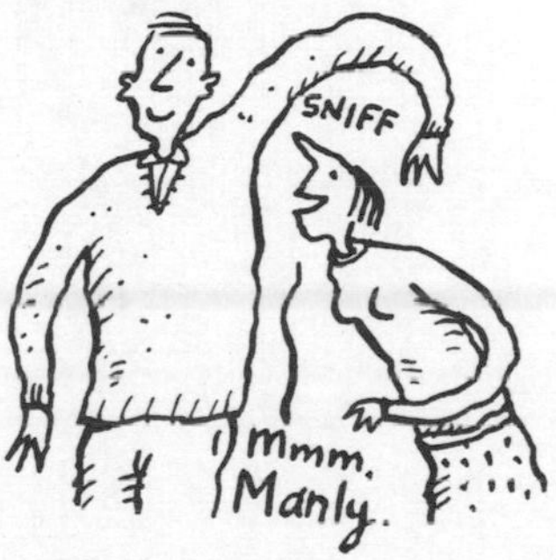
SNIFF
Mmm. Manly.

SLOBBISH BEHAVIOUR:

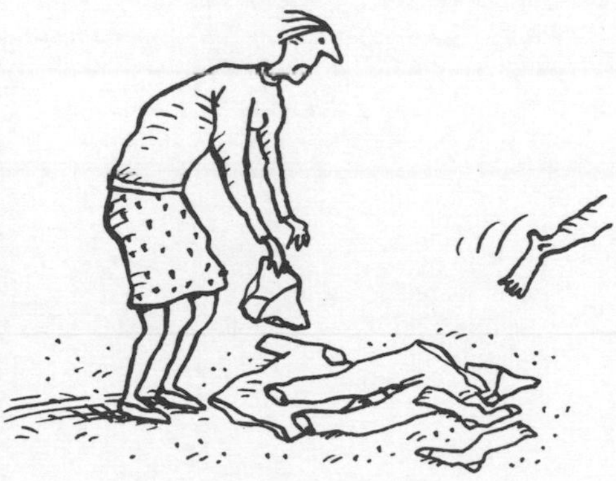

BEING HYPOCRITICAL:

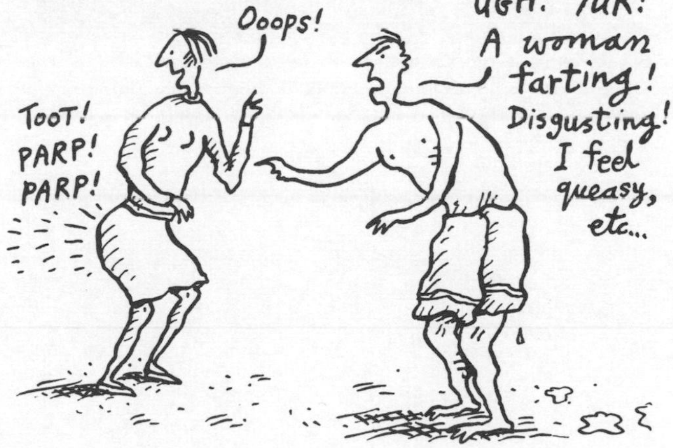
Ooops!
TOOT!
PARP!
PARP!
UGH! YUK! A woman farting! Disgusting! I feel queasy, etc...

LOVE OF CROWDS

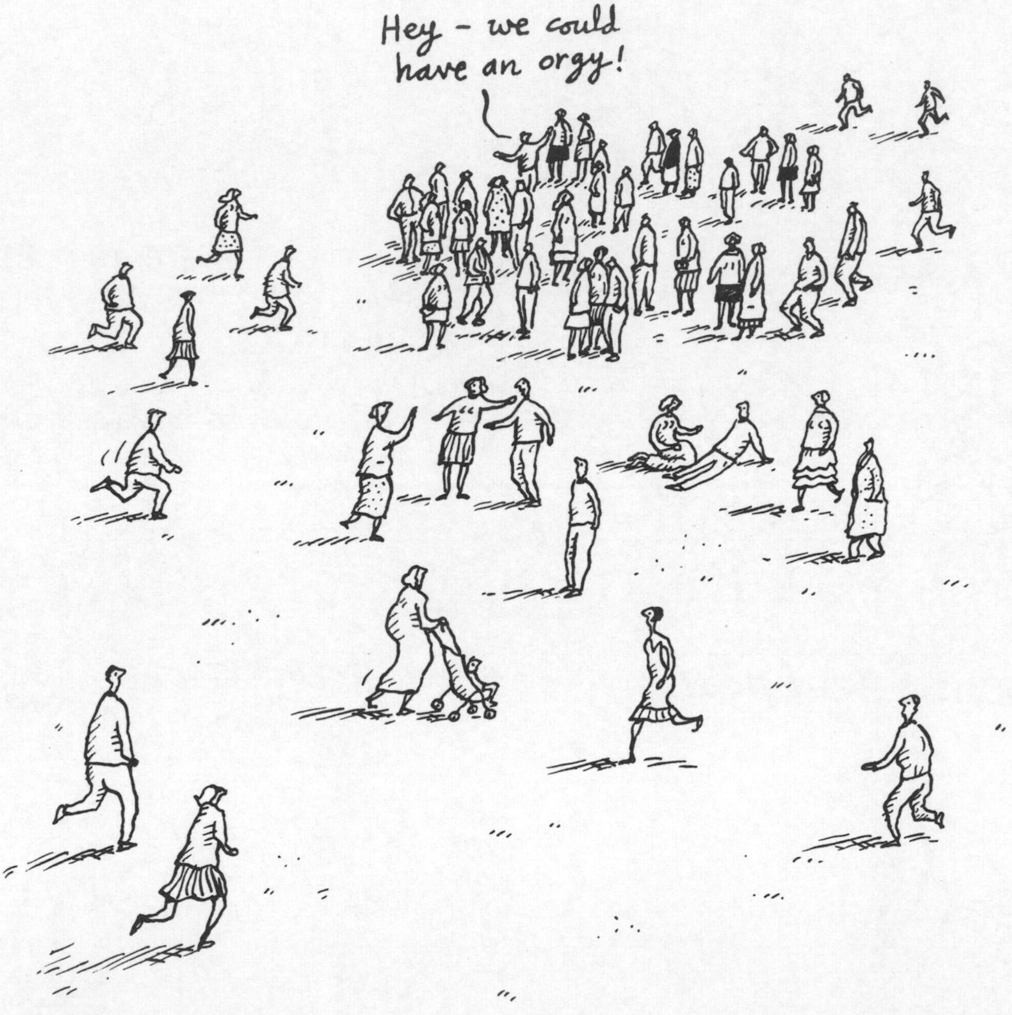
Hey - we could have an orgy!

LOVE OF BEING ALONE

THE **OBJECT** OF YOUR **LOVE**.

Falling in love with a human being can be emotionally draining, so sometimes it's safer to love THINGS rather than people. THINGS don't have a mind of their own. They can't behave unpredictably, they won't bite and they won't take offence or judge you harshly if and when you discard them for a later model. Here are some loyal THINGS which won't let you down...

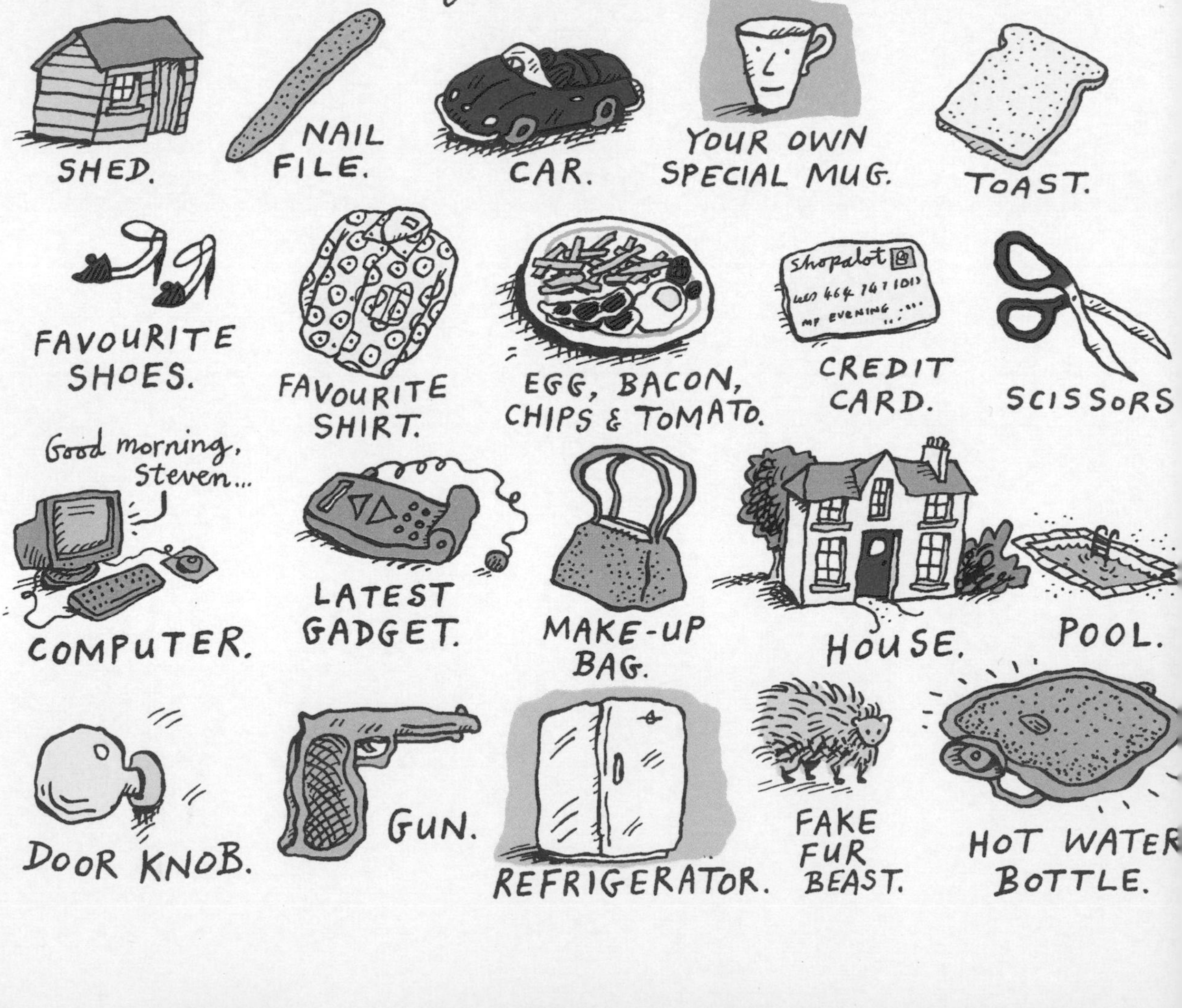
SHED.
NAIL FILE.
CAR.
YOUR OWN SPECIAL MUG.
TOAST.
FAVOURITE SHOES.
FAVOURITE SHIRT.
EGG, BACON, CHIPS & TOMATO.
Shopalot
CREDIT CARD.
SCISSORS
Good morning, Steven...
COMPUTER.
LATEST GADGET.
MAKE-UP BAG.
HOUSE.
POOL.
DOOR KNOB.
GUN.
REFRIGERATOR.
FAKE FUR BEAST.
HOT WATER BOTTLE.

3

FALLING IN LOVE

Whatever sex of person you fall in love with, here are some of the ways it may happen...

i - LOVE AT FIRST SIGHT
(careful not to confuse it with LUST at first sight):

PING! PING!

ii - LOVE AT THIRTY-FIRST SIGHT:

Have you seen the stapler?

It's... er... gosh... I seem... to... to LOVE you!

iii - LOVE AT FIRST CONVERSATION:

Do you find potatoes interesting?

No.

Well, neither do I!

iv - HATE AT FIRST SIGHT
(turning, incredulously for all concerned, to LOVE later on):

I HATE you!

And I HATE you! But I can't live WITHOUT you!

v - FRIENDSHIP TURNING SLOWLY TO LOVE:

Familiarity has bred, not contempt, but LOVE.

vi - LUST & MAD, PASSIONATE SEX turning, upon waking up one sunny morning, to LOVE:

I... I LOVE you...

What's your name?

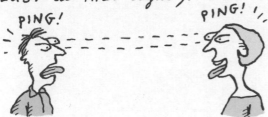

vii- LOVE AT A DISTANCE:

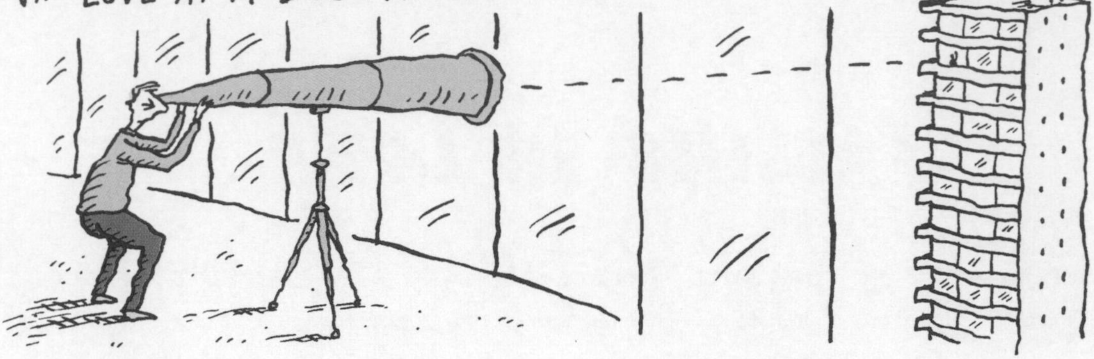

viii- SHARED ACTIVITIES & HOBBIES turning to LOVE:

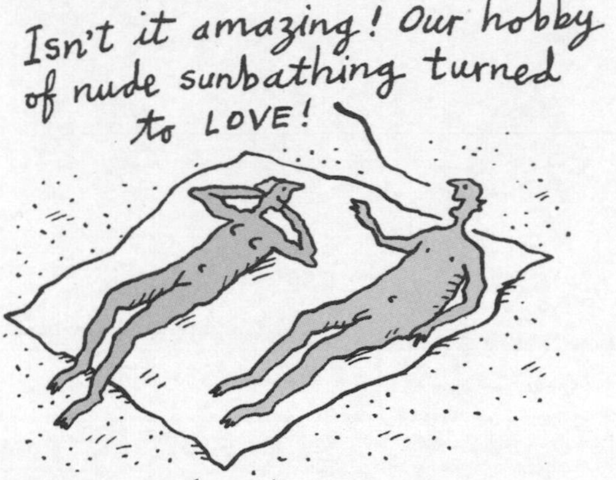
Isn't it amazing! Our hobby of nude sunbathing turned to LOVE!

ix- TAKING OFF ONE ANOTHER'S GLASSES turning to LOVE:

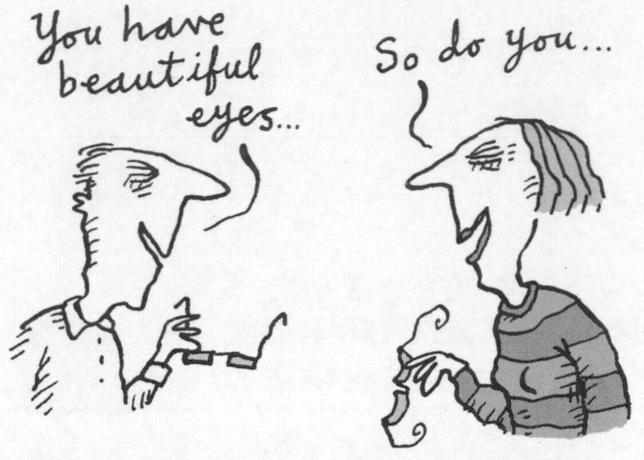
You have beautiful eyes...
So do you...

x- MEETING ON THE BUS FOR 25 YEARS turning to LOVE:

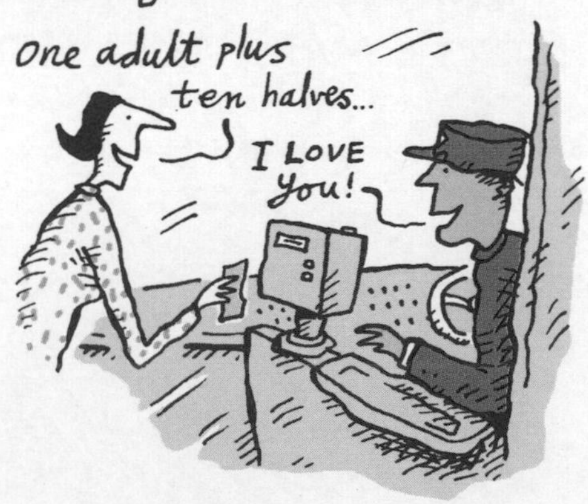
One adult plus ten halves...
I LOVE you!

xi- LOVE FOR THE OLDER WOMAN - a man subconsciously searching for a MOTHER FIGURE:

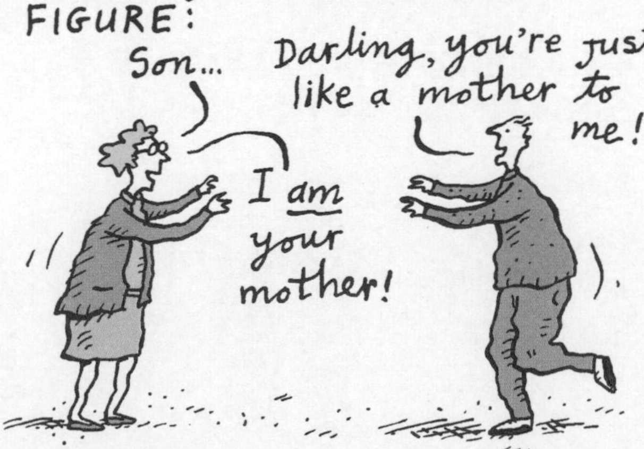
Son...
Darling, you're just like a mother to me!
I am your mother!

FALLING IN LOVE – A CASE STUDY

Sometimes we don't show ourselves to our best advantage...

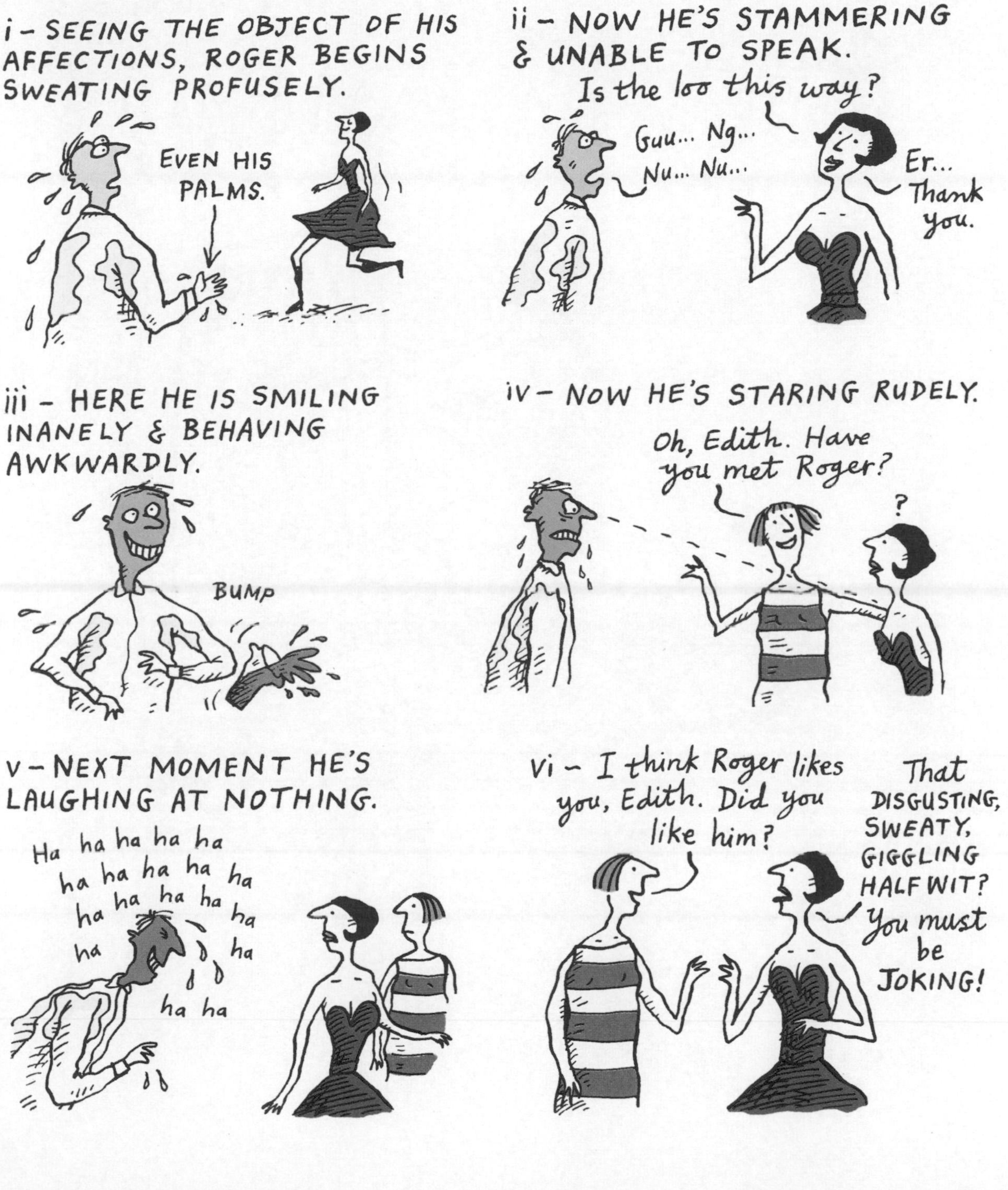
i – SEEING THE OBJECT OF HIS AFFECTIONS, ROGER BEGINS SWEATING PROFUSELY.
EVEN HIS PALMS.
ii – NOW HE'S STAMMERING & UNABLE TO SPEAK.
Is the loo this way?
Guu... Ng... Nu... Nu...
Er... Thank you.
iii – HERE HE IS SMILING INANELY & BEHAVING AWKWARDLY.
BUMP
iv – NOW HE'S STARING RUDELY.
Oh, Edith. Have you met Roger?
?
v – NEXT MOMENT HE'S LAUGHING AT NOTHING.
Ha ha ha ha ha ha ha ha ha ha ha ha ha ha ha ha ha ha ha ha ha
vi – I think Roger likes you, Edith. Did you like him?
That DISGUSTING, SWEATY, GIGGLING HALFWIT? You must be JOKING!

THE RITUALS OF STARTING A NEW RELATIONSHIP:

Number 1 ~ HIM

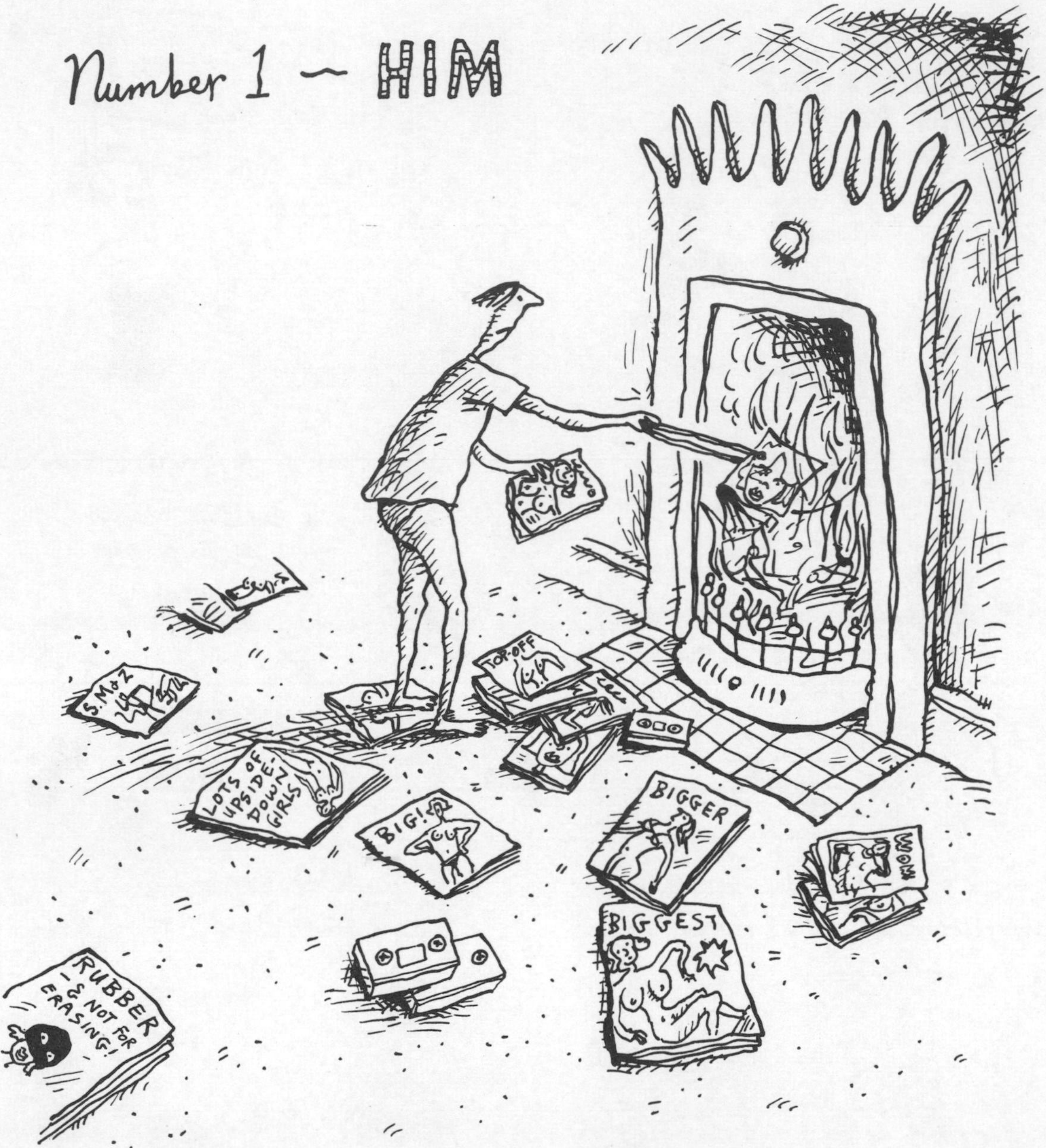
TOP-OFF
LOTS OF UPSIDE-DOWN GIRLS
BIG!
BIGGER
WOW
BIGGEST
RUBBER IS NOT FOR ERASING!

BURNING HIS PORNOGRAPHY COLLECTION.

WHY NOT HELP THINGS ALONG by cutting out these **POSTCARDS** and sending them to YOUR loved one...

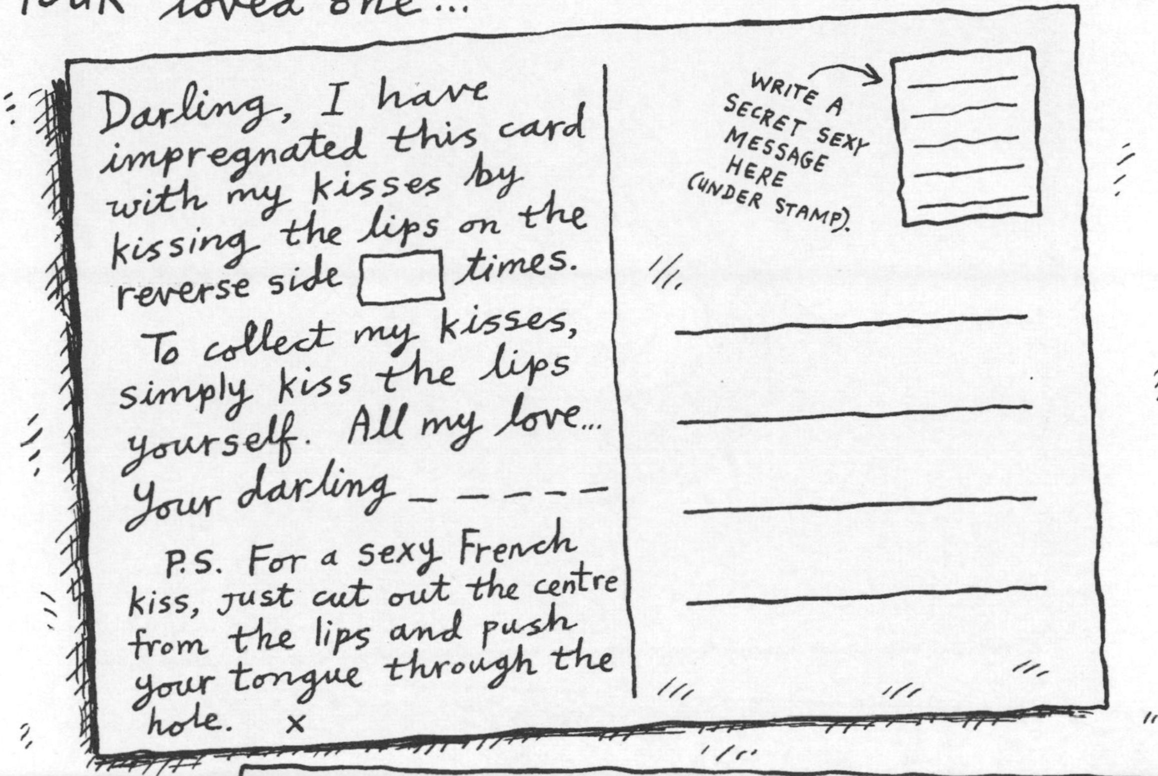
Darling, I have impregnated this card with my kisses by kissing the lips on the reverse side [ ] times.
To collect my kisses, simply kiss the lips yourself. All my love...
Your darling _ _ _ _ _
P.S. For a sexy French kiss, just cut out the centre from the lips and push your tongue through the hole. x
WRITE A SECRET SEXY MESSAGE HERE (UNDER STAMP).

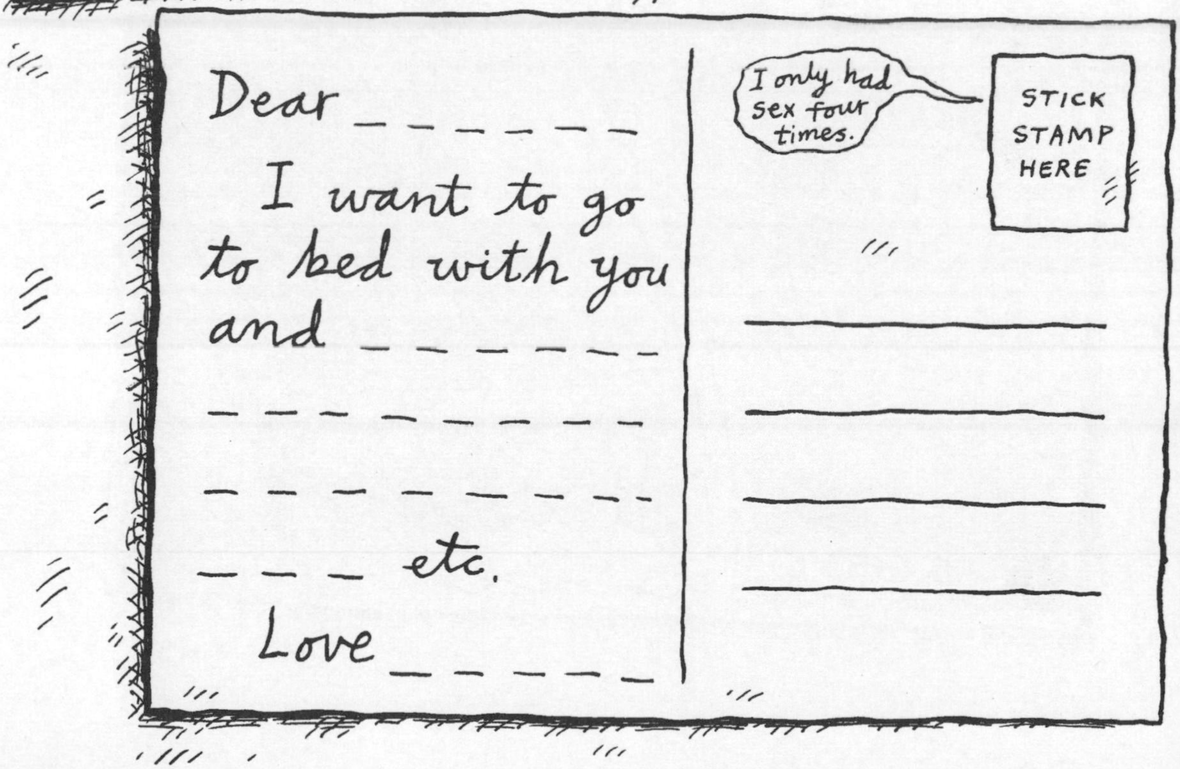
Dear _ _ _ _ _ _ _
I want to go to bed with you and _ _ _ _ _ _
_ _ _ _ _ _ _ _ _
_ _ _ _ _ _ _ _ _
_ _ _ _ etc.
Love _ _ _ _ _ _
I only had sex four times.
STICK STAMP HERE

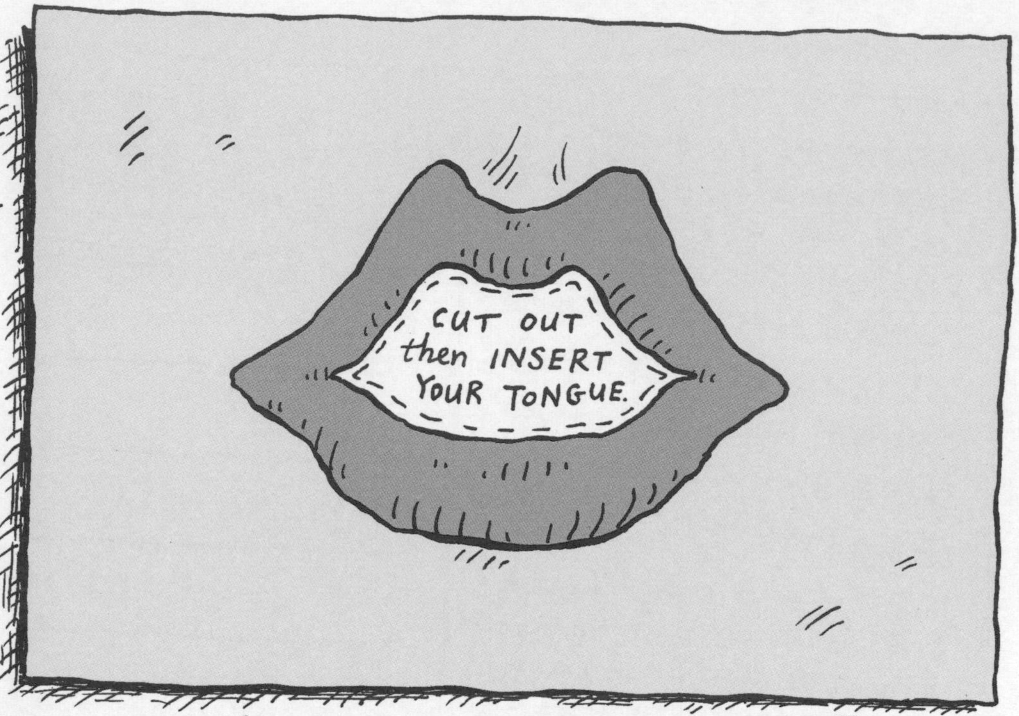
CUT OUT
then INSERT
YOUR TONGUE.

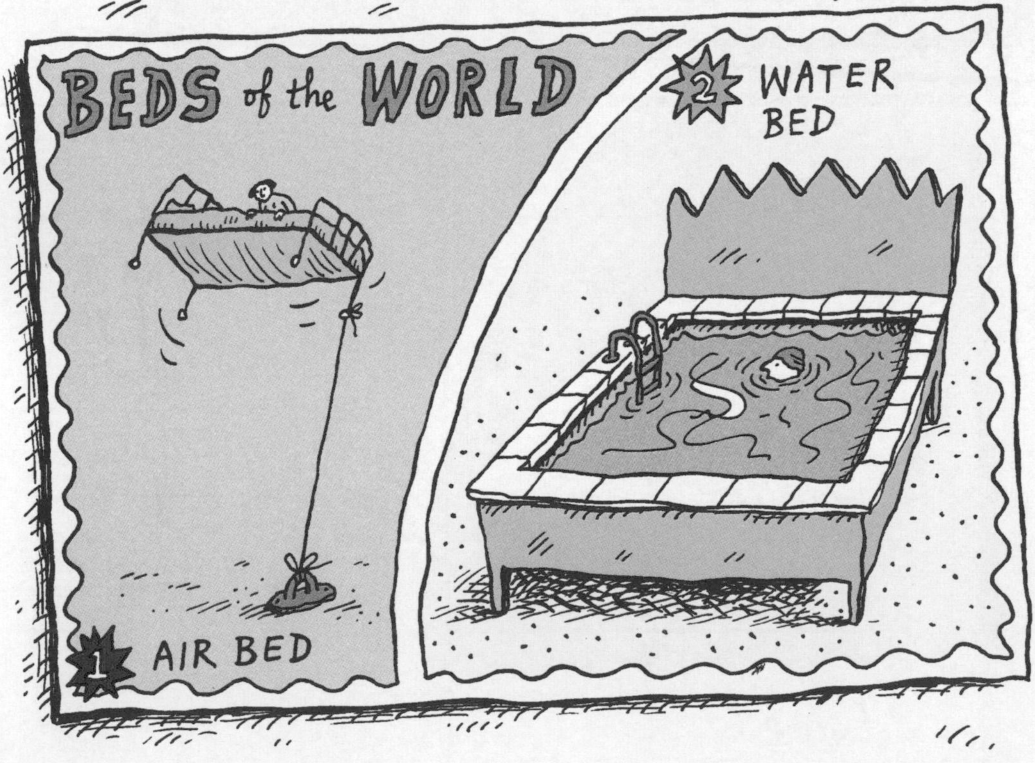
BEDS of the WORLD
1 AIR BED
2 WATER BED

CHOOSING between more than one SUITOR

If you are a princess, you'll probably come across this problem quite often. The rest of us aren't so lucky, but just in case here are a few of the classic solutions...

TELL THEM TO FIGHT TO THE DEATH:

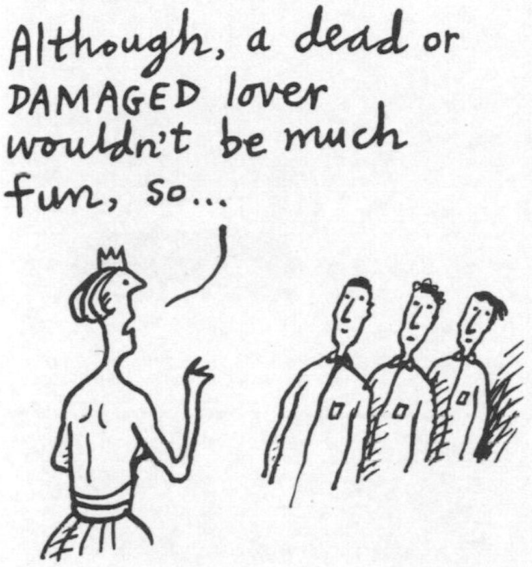

Although, a dead or DAMAGED lover wouldn't be much fun, so...

SET THEM A QUEST:

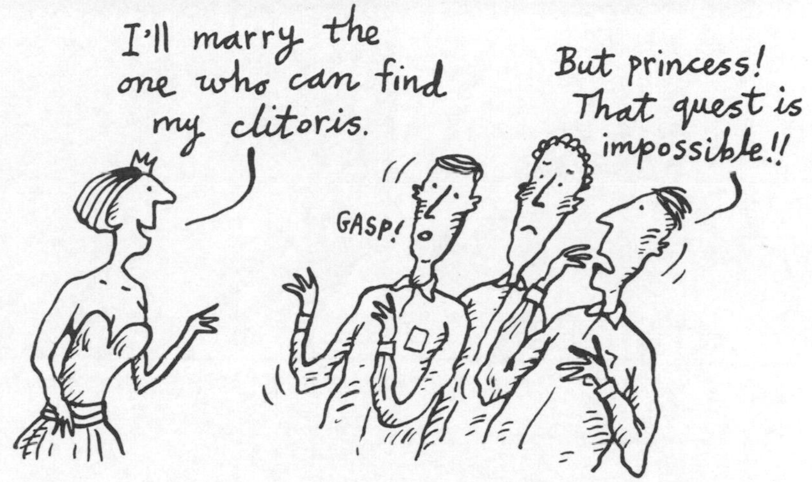

I'll marry the one who can find my clitoris.
GASP!
But princess! That quest is impossible!!

HOW ABOUT A STRAIGHT SIZE COMPARISON?

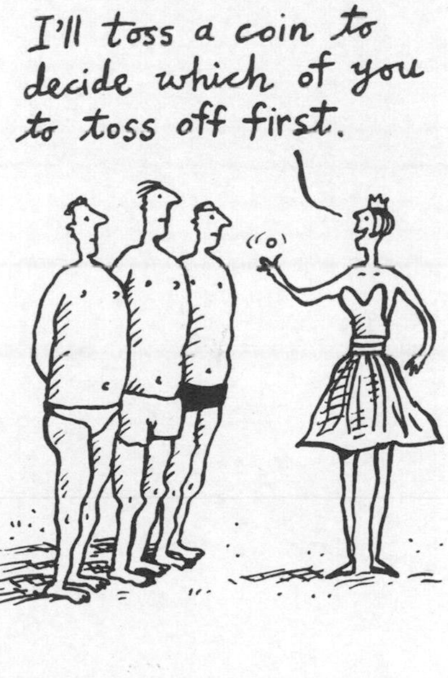

I'll toss a coin to decide which of you to toss off first.

FIND OUT WHO HAS THE MOST MONEY:

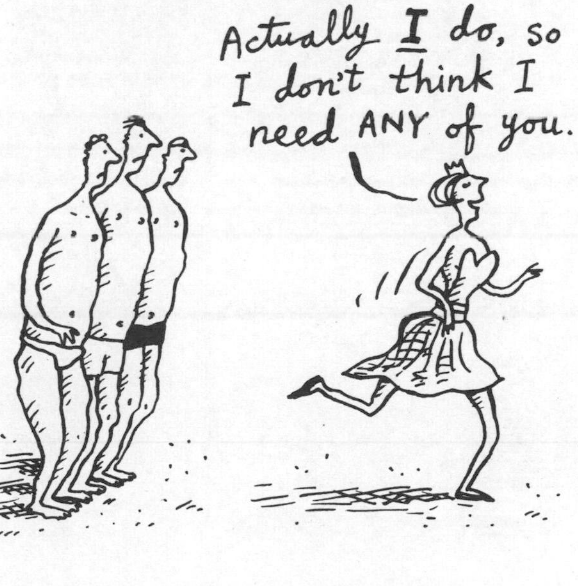

Actually I do, so I don't think I need ANY of you.

THE UPs

When you have successfully fallen in love, it will be helpful to know what to expect. Here are some of love's effects...

LOVE MAKES THE SUN SHINE... Even on a rainy day.

THE MOON GLOW...

AND COLOURS BLAZE. My red car is on fire!

LOVE MAKES YOU SAY NICE THINGS. You were wonderful. So were you.

LOVE MAKES ALL YOUR ACHES & PAINS GO AWAY. It releases your endorphins. LEAP

LOVE LETS YOU TOLERATE ANYTHING. I even love waiting for our delayed plane with you.

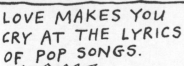

LOVE MAKES YOU CRY AT THE LYRICS OF POP SONGS. She loves you, YEAH! YEAH! YEAH! So true! (SIGH)

LOVE MAKES YOU HAPPY. FULL UP WITH LOVE.

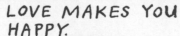

LOVE MAKES PROBLEMS SEEM INSIGNIFICANT. Your willie is tiny but I don't mind.

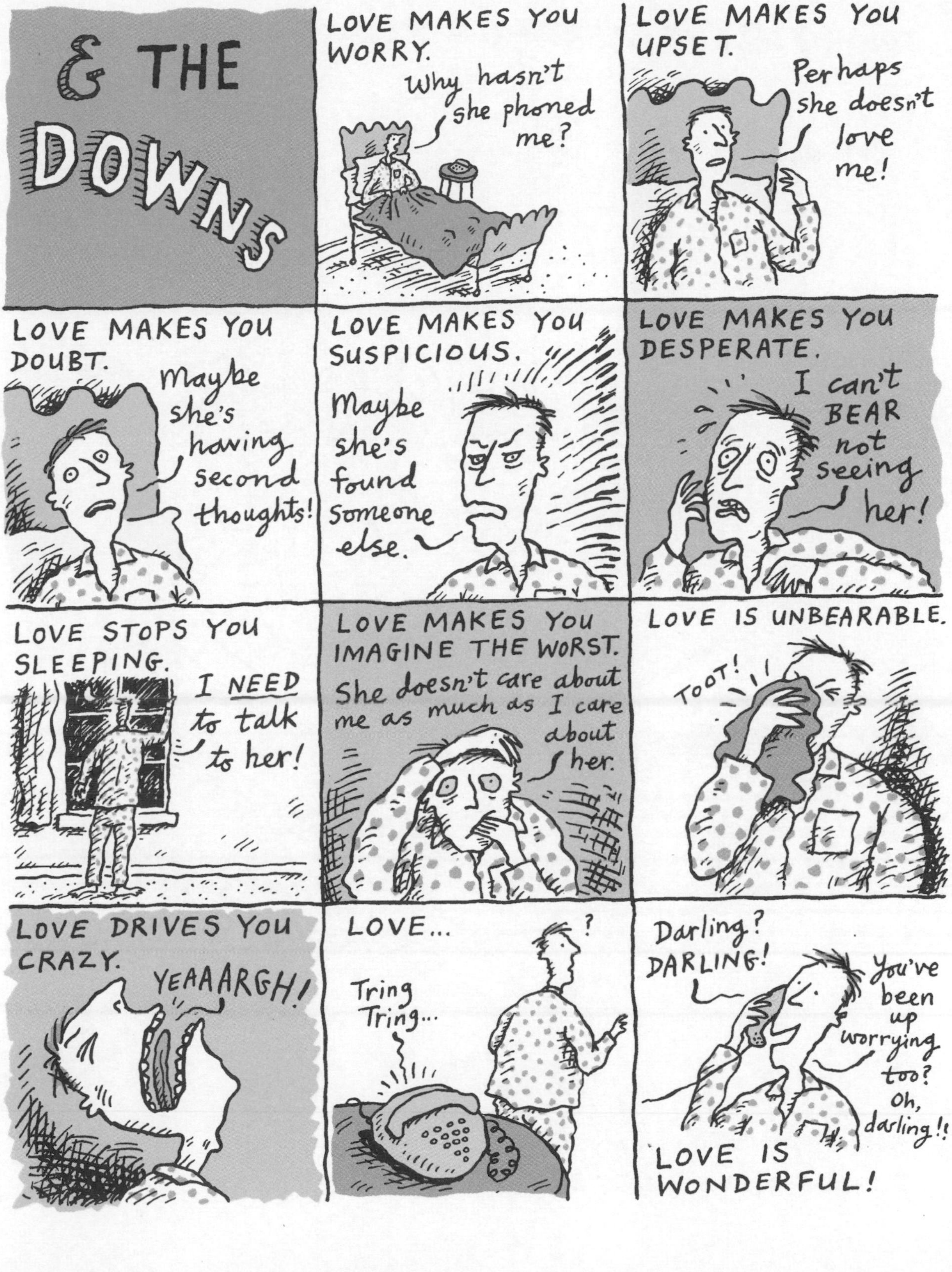
& THE DOWNS
LOVE MAKES YOU WORRY.
Why hasn't she phoned me?
LOVE MAKES YOU UPSET.
Perhaps she doesn't love me!
LOVE MAKES YOU DOUBT.
Maybe she's having second thoughts!
LOVE MAKES YOU SUSPICIOUS.
Maybe she's found someone else.
LOVE MAKES YOU DESPERATE.
I can't BEAR not seeing her!
LOVE STOPS YOU SLEEPING.
I NEED to talk to her!
LOVE MAKES YOU IMAGINE THE WORST.
She doesn't care about me as much as I care about her.
LOVE IS UNBEARABLE.
TOOT!
LOVE DRIVES YOU CRAZY.
YEAAARGH!
LOVE...
?
Tring Tring...
Darling? DARLING!
You've been up worrying too? Oh, darling!!
LOVE IS WONDERFUL!

THE RITUALS OF STARTING A NEW RELATIONSHIP:

Number 2 ~ HER

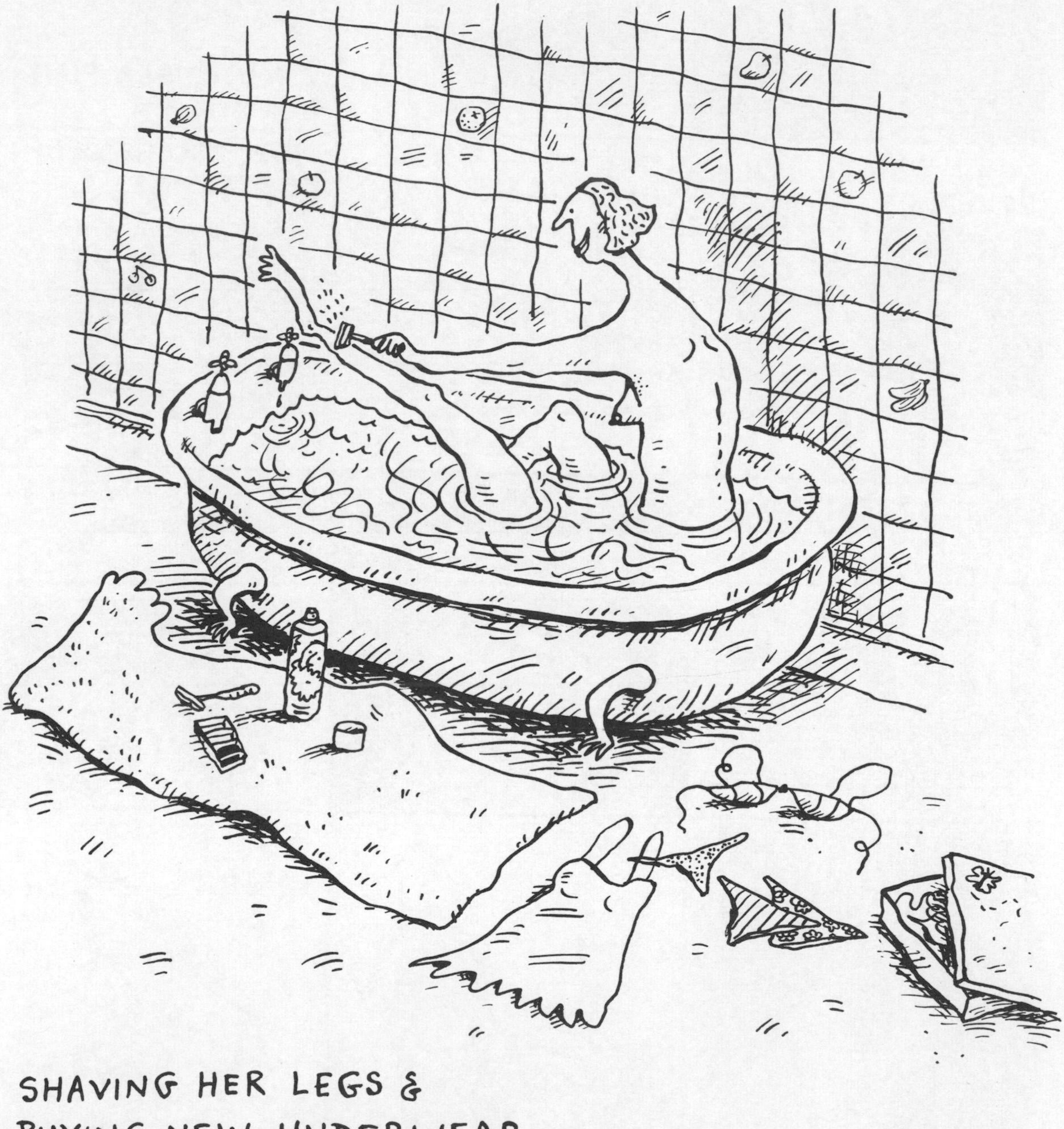

SHAVING HER LEGS & BUYING NEW UNDERWEAR.

OF COURSE, it's a well-known fact that

LOVE ADDLES THE BRAIN

Here we see otherwise perfectly sane and sensible people talking to each other in BABY TALK!

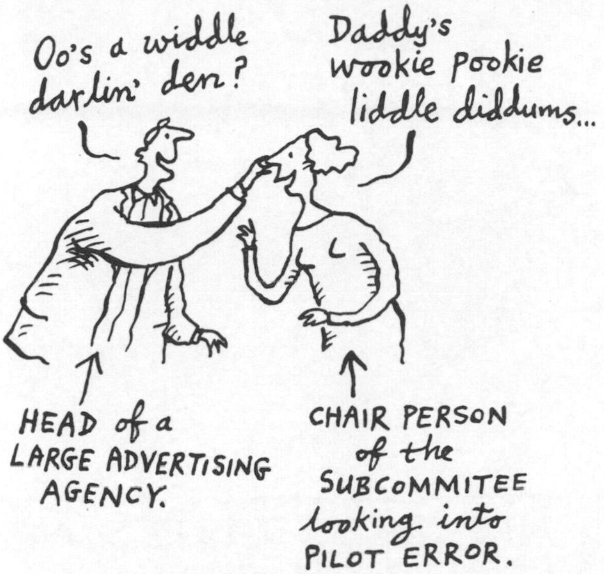
Oo's a widdle darlin' den?
Daddy's wookie pookie liddle diddums...
HEAD of a LARGE ADVERTISING AGENCY.
CHAIR PERSON of the SUBCOMMITEE looking into PILOT ERROR.

BUYING EACH OTHER PINK FLUFFY SOFT TOYS...

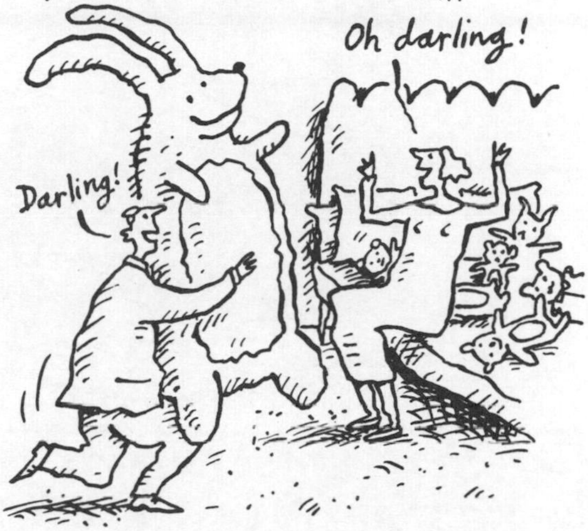
Oh darling!
Darling!

AND CALLING EACH OTHER PET NAMES <u>IN</u> <u>PUBLIC!!</u>

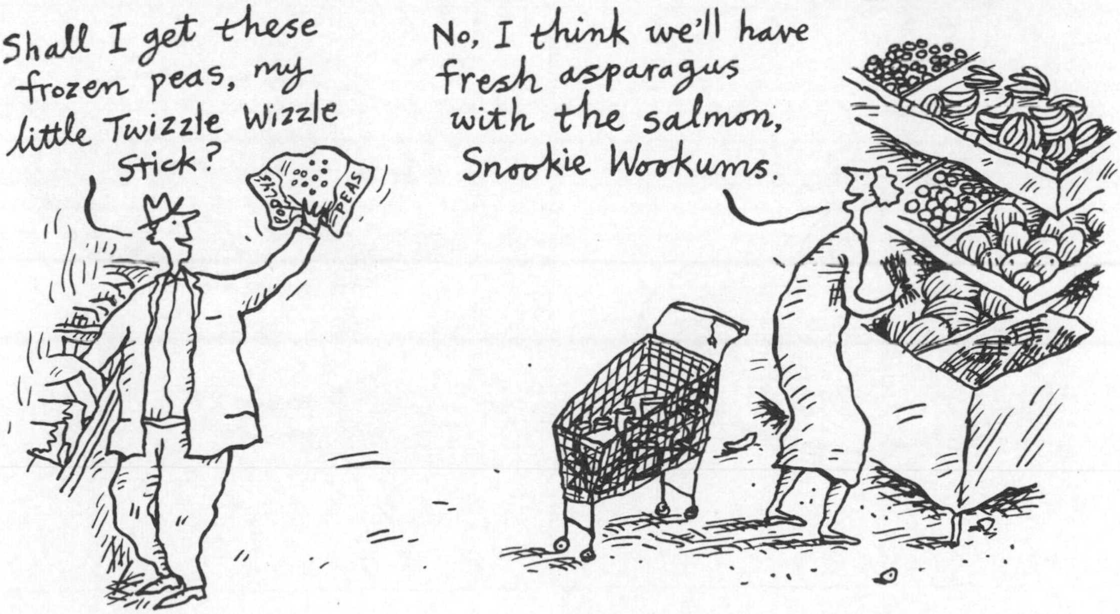
Shall I get these frozen peas, my little Twizzle Wizzle Stick?
No, I think we'll have fresh asparagus with the salmon, Snookie Wookums.
PEAS

If you love someone enough to

EAT THEM UP

here are a few suggestions...

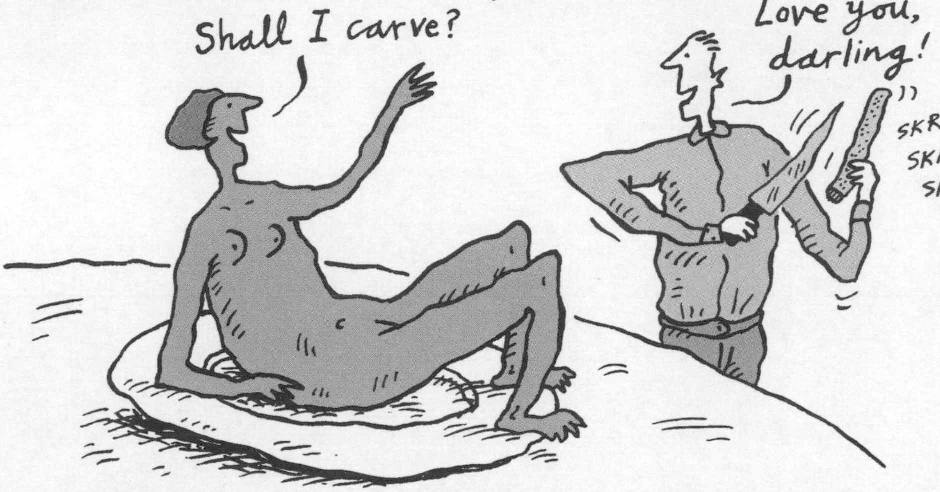
Shall I carve?
Love you, darling!
SKRIK
SKRIK
SKRIK

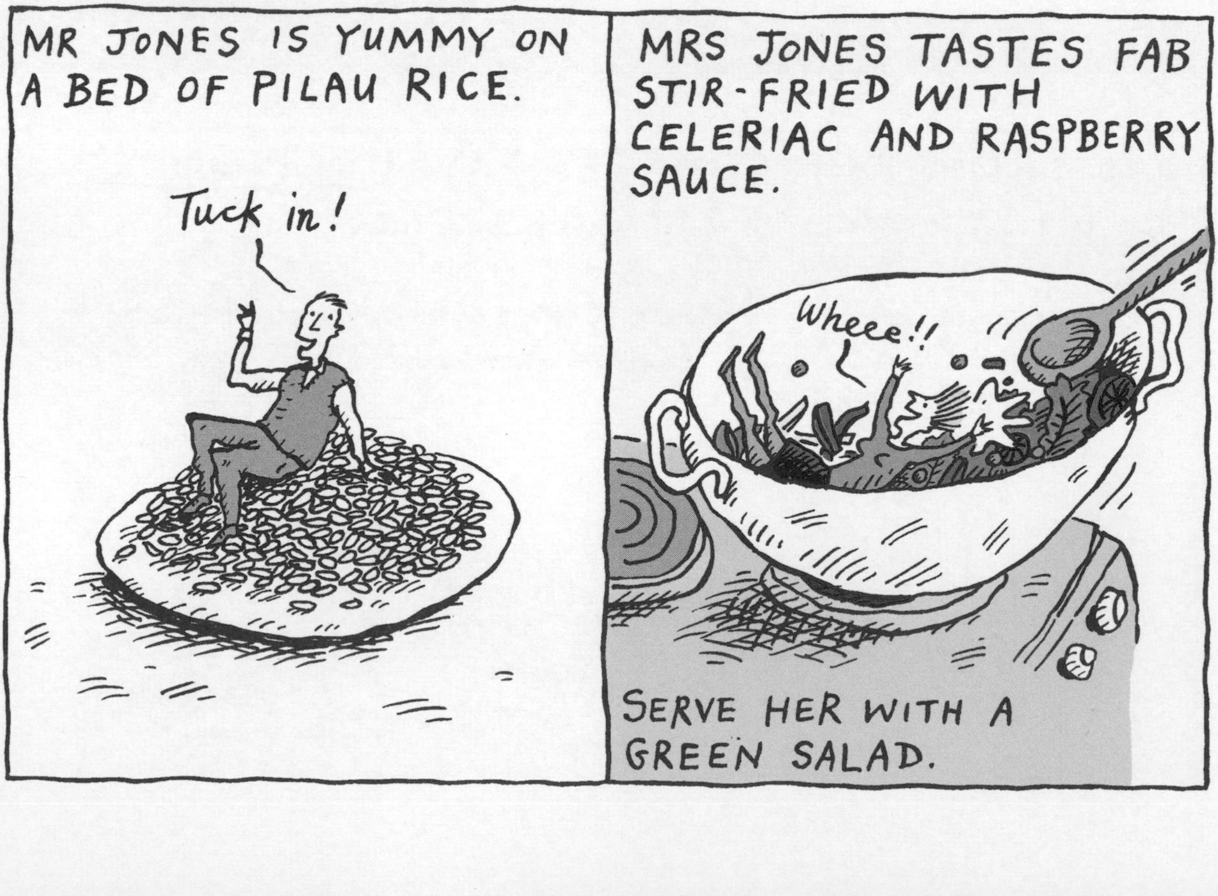
MR JONES IS YUMMY ON A BED OF PILAU RICE.
Tuck in!
MRS JONES TASTES FAB STIR-FRIED WITH CELERIAC AND RASPBERRY SAUCE.
Wheee!!
SERVE HER WITH A GREEN SALAD.

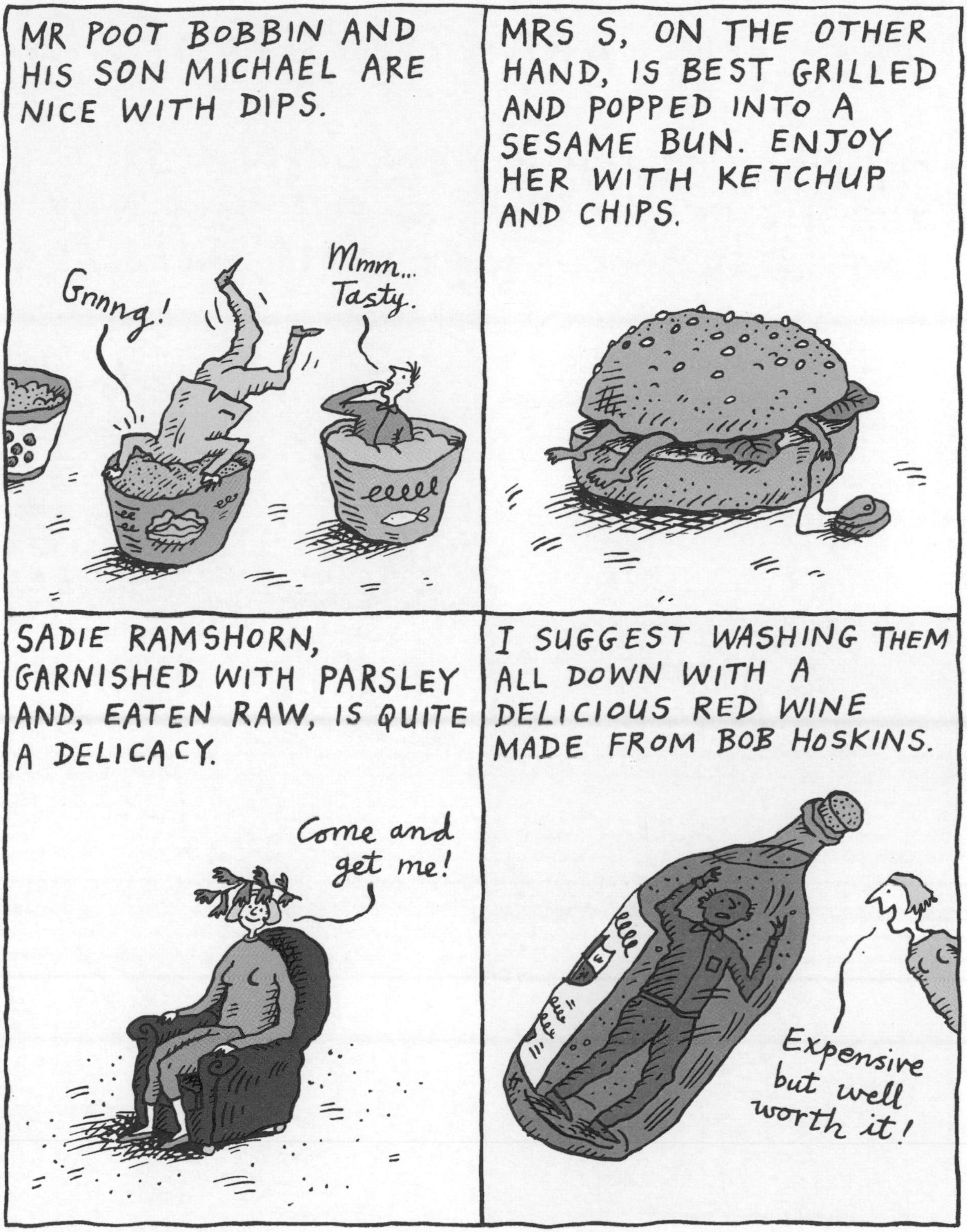
MR POOT BOBBIN AND HIS SON MICHAEL ARE NICE WITH DIPS.
Gnnng!
Mmm... Tasty.
MRS S, ON THE OTHER HAND, IS BEST GRILLED AND POPPED INTO A SESAME BUN. ENJOY HER WITH KETCHUP AND CHIPS.
SADIE RAMSHORN, GARNISHED WITH PARSLEY AND, EATEN RAW, IS QUITE A DELICACY.
Come and get me!
I SUGGEST WASHING THEM ALL DOWN WITH A DELICIOUS RED WINE MADE FROM BOB HOSKINS.
Expensive but well worth it!

TALKING ABOUT YOURSELF...

The FIRST FLUSH of NEW LOVE is JUST THE RIGHT MOMENT to tell <u>your</u> NEW LOVE about some of your WORST EXCESSES!

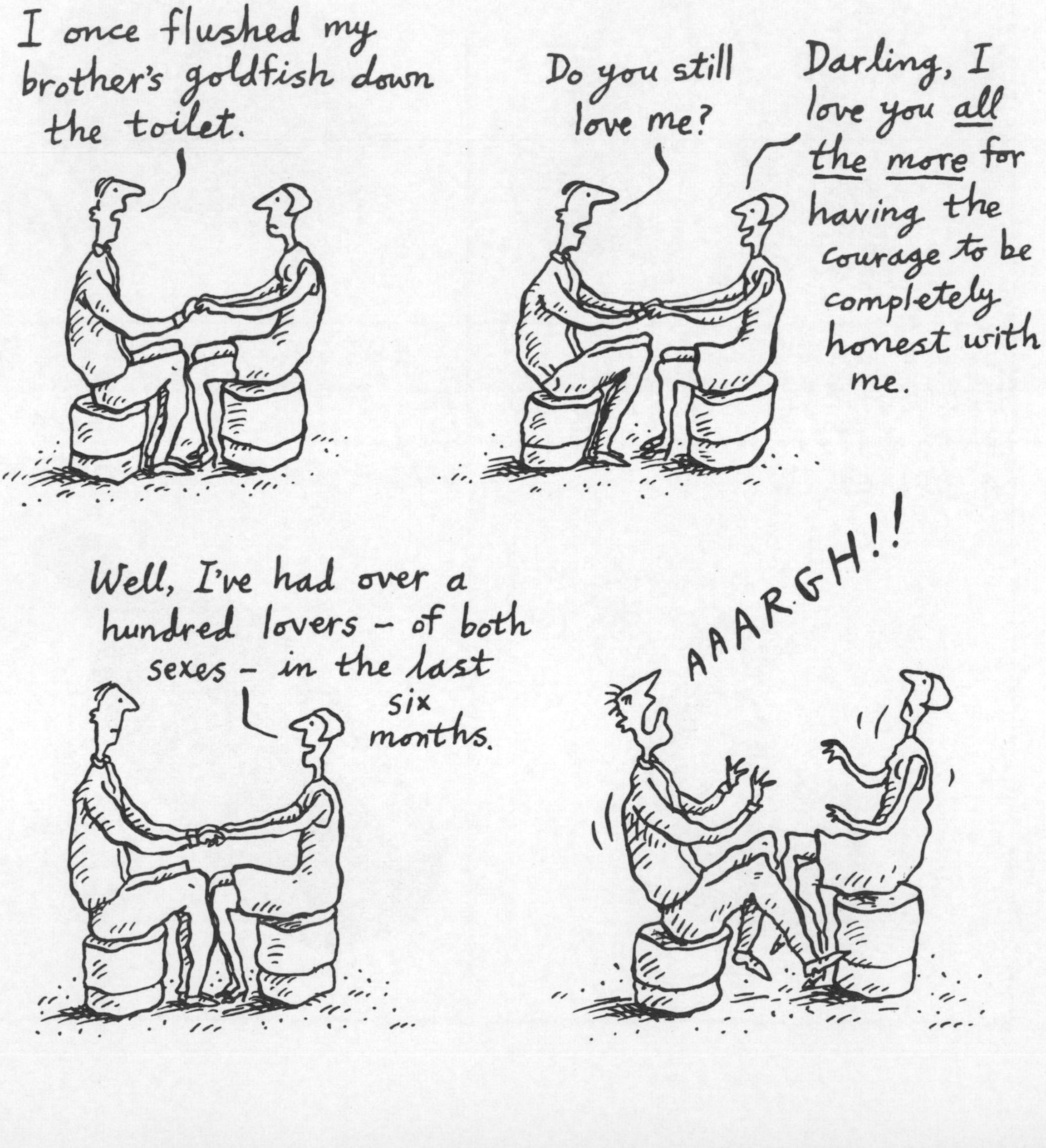
I once flushed my brother's goldfish down the toilet.
Do you still love me?
Darling, I love you all the more for having the courage to be completely honest with me.
Well, I've had over a hundred lovers - of both sexes - in the last six months.
AAARGH!!

Despite ALL the TALKING you can do, EVERY HUMAN BEING is an ISLAND and it is IMPOSSIBLE to know EXACTLY what he or she REALLY THINKS... unless you understand

HOW TO INTERPRET BODY LANGUAGE

TOUCHING YOUR KNEE:  Means absolutely nothing – except that you are friends.	**HOLDING HANDS:**  Again, virtually meaningless – but nice.	**KISSING YOU ON THE CHEEK:**  Meaningless if you are a business acquaintance. If you are lovers, it means it's all over.
PUTTING HIS OR HER TONGUE IN YOUR MOUTH:  She – or he – likes you.	**ASKING YOU TO WALK HIM OR HER HOME:**  Hard to say. Maybe just afraid of the dark. Unless it's still daylight...	**OFFERING YOU A CUP OF COFFEE OR A BANANA:**  This is probably some kind of code – but it's unintelligible to me.
KISSING YOUR BELLY BUTTON:  Just good – VERY good – friends.	**UNDOING YOUR TROUSERS:**  Did you spill something on them? If not, it could be significant.	**PUTTING A CONDOM ON YOUR WILLIE:**  There's only one conclusion to be reached here. Probably...

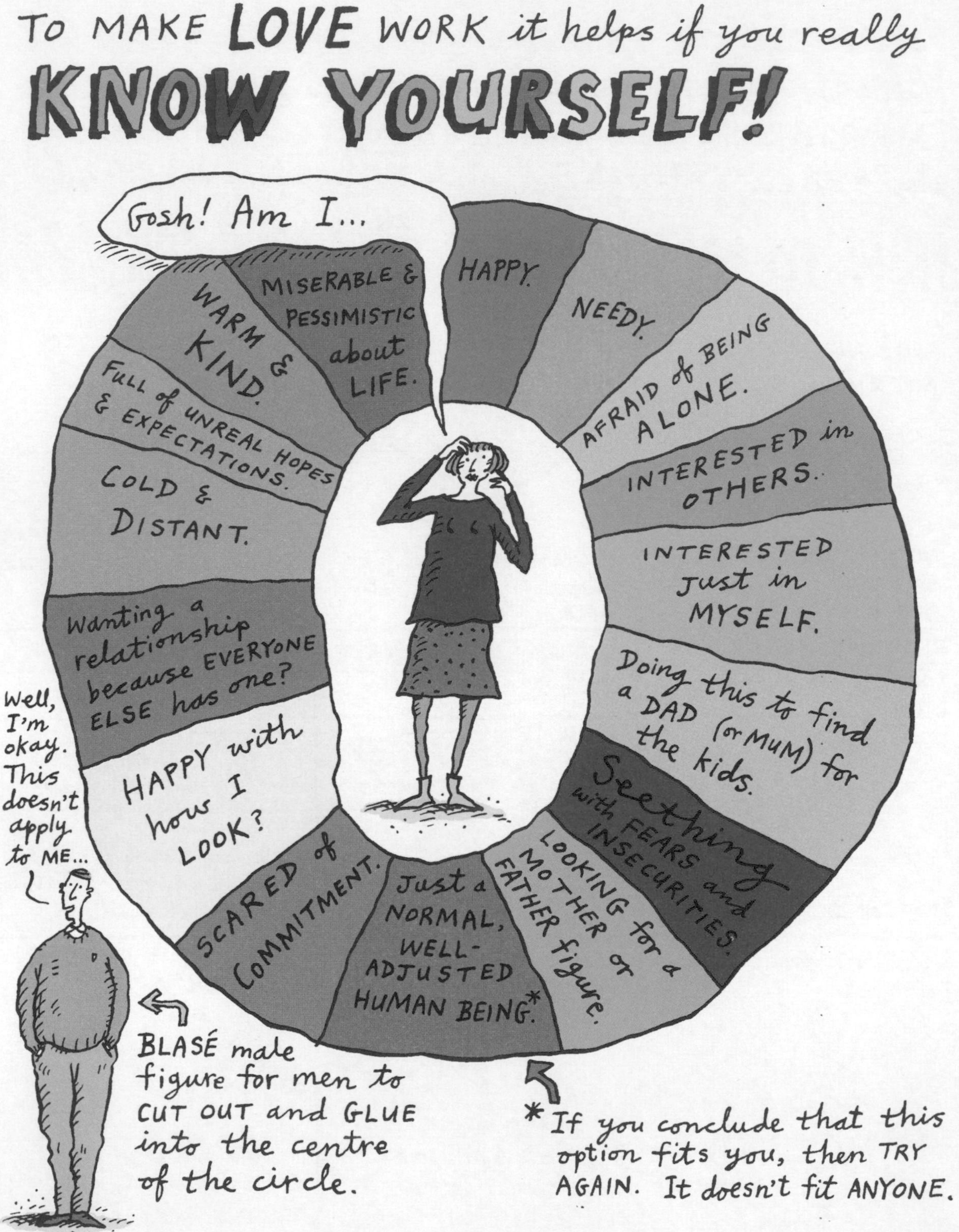
TO MAKE LOVE WORK it helps if you really
KNOW YOURSELF!
Gosh! Am I...
MISERABLE & PESSIMISTIC about LIFE.
HAPPY.
NEEDY.
AFRAID of BEING ALONE.
INTERESTED in OTHERS.
INTERESTED Just in MYSELF.
Doing this to find a DAD (or MUM) for the kids.
Seething with FEARS and INSECURITIES.
LOOKING for a MOTHER or FATHER figure.
Just a NORMAL, WELL-ADJUSTED HUMAN BEING.*
SCARED of COMMITMENT.
HAPPY with how I LOOK?
Wanting a relationship because EVERYONE ELSE has one?
COLD & DISTANT.
FULL of UNREAL HOPES & EXPECTATIONS.
WARM & KIND.
Well, I'm okay. This doesn't apply to ME...
BLASÉ male figure for men to CUT OUT and GLUE into the centre of the circle.
* If you conclude that this option fits you, then TRY AGAIN. It doesn't fit ANYONE.

SOONER or LATER the TIME WILL COME to say...

"I LOVE YOU"

Too soon, and it can scare your prospective partner off. Too late and they are off anyway. Here are some ways of saying 'I love you' to beware of:

① Come on! Say 'I love you'!

HAVING TO PROMPT IS BAD NEWS.

② I... ghak... uk... gnaah... yuh...

HE'S CHOKING OVER THE WORDS. GIVE HIM A WIDE BERTH.

③ I LOVE you! And you... And you... And you...

HERE, IT'S COMING OUT TOO EASILY.

④ I love you SO MUCH I'm going to KILL myself!

THIS IS TOO MELODRAMATIC.

⑤ Say 'I love you'! Define 'LOVE...'

THIS PARTNER IS TOO ANALYTICAL.

A SMALL **WIND-DRIVEN LOVE** CATCHER

CUT OUT the many parts. Assemble EXACTLY according to the NUMERICAL SYSTEM. Hang above your bed. The carefully designed shapes capture LOVE PARTICLES drifting free in the atmosphere and, via the sophisticated reflecting panels, bounce them down onto the people occupying the bed. Magnifies LOVE and enhances SEXUAL PLEASURE.

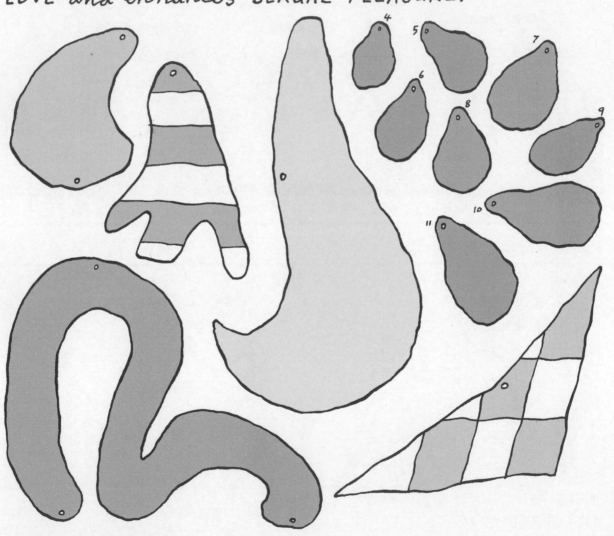

If YOUR life lacks LOVE, you'll be AMAZED by the results when using this device!

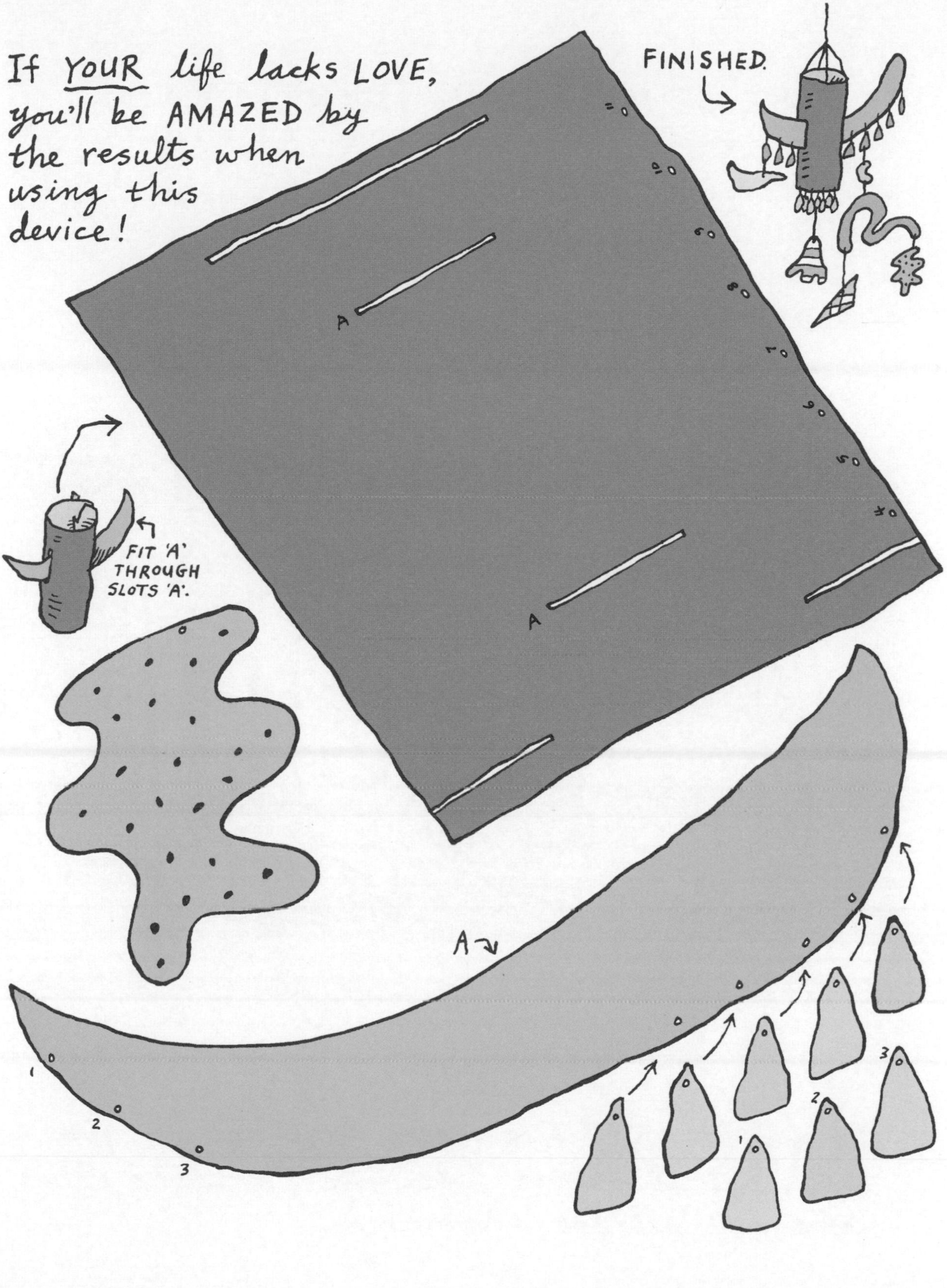

FINISHED.
A
A
FIT 'A' THROUGH SLOTS 'A'.
A
1
2
3
1
2
3

A CASE OF MISTAKEN IDENTITY...

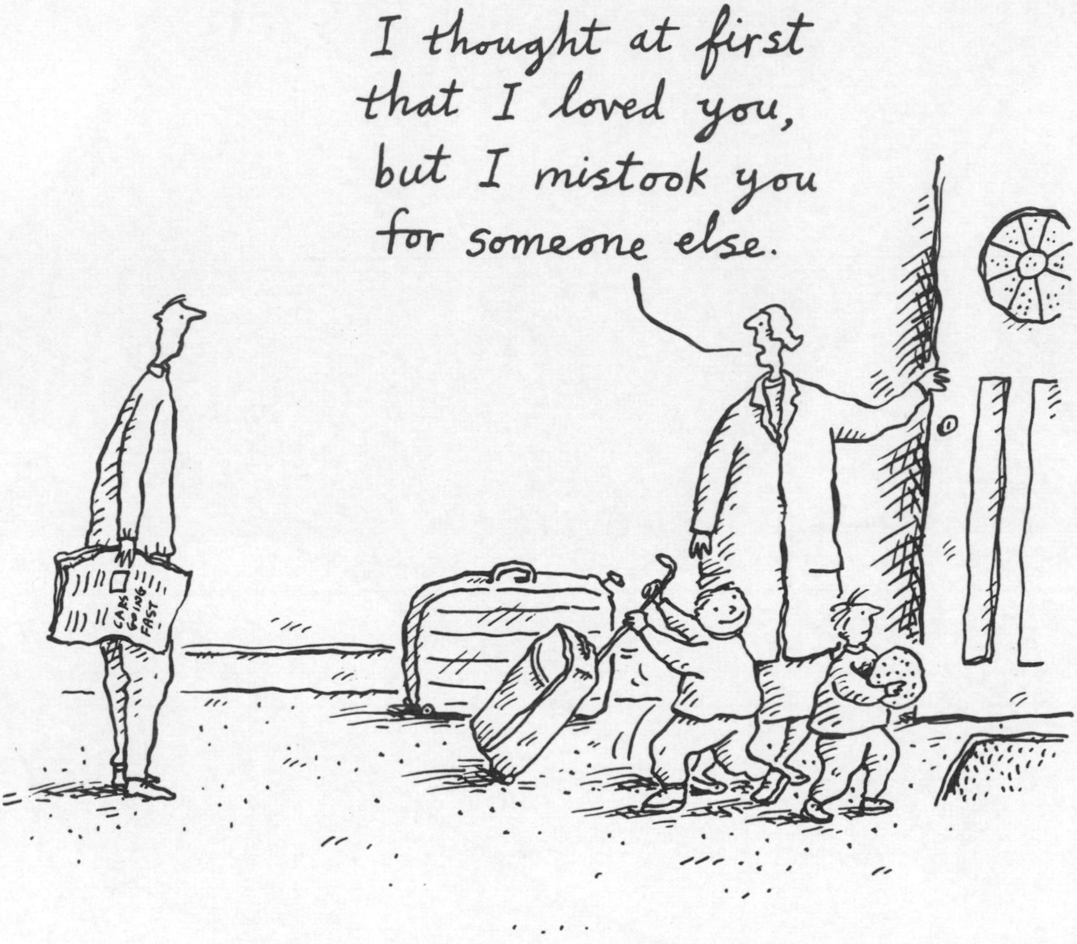
I thought at first that I loved you, but I mistook you for someone else.
CARS GOING FAST

Mr and Mrs K. have been together for five years, but it seems like five thousand. This scenario is all too common.

IMPRESSIVE WAYS TO SAY 'I LOVE YOU'

Which of these examples is the most heroic, thus making it the most appreciated?

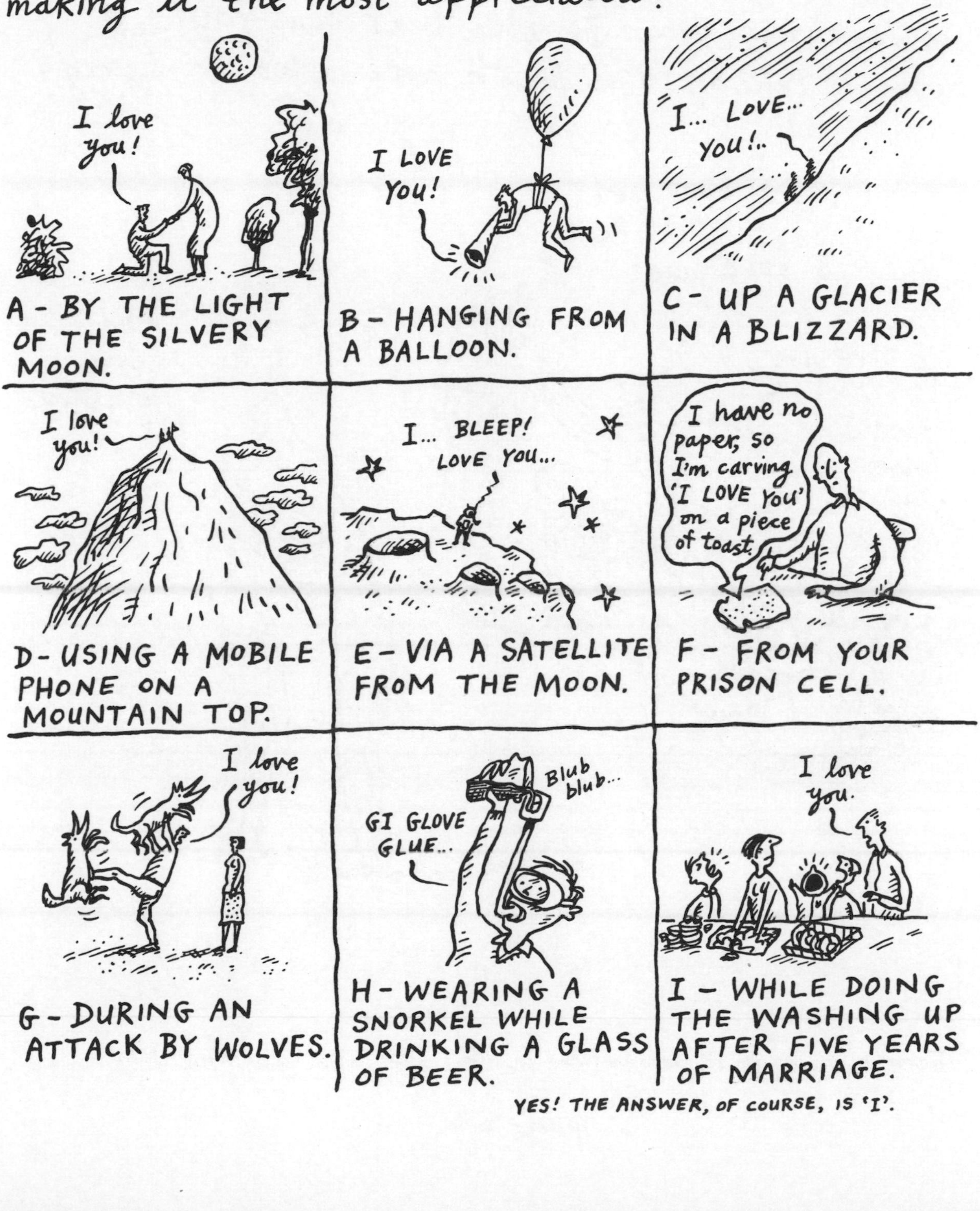
I love you!
A - BY THE LIGHT OF THE SILVERY MOON.
I LOVE YOU!
B - HANGING FROM A BALLOON.
I... LOVE... YOU!..
C - UP A GLACIER IN A BLIZZARD.
I love you!
D - USING A MOBILE PHONE ON A MOUNTAIN TOP.
I... BLEEP! LOVE YOU...
E - VIA A SATELLITE FROM THE MOON.
I have no paper, so I'm carving 'I LOVE YOU' on a piece of toast.
F - FROM YOUR PRISON CELL.
I love you!
G - DURING AN ATTACK BY WOLVES.
Blub blub...
GI GLOVE GLUE...
H - WEARING A SNORKEL WHILE DRINKING A GLASS OF BEER.
I love you.
I - WHILE DOING THE WASHING UP AFTER FIVE YEARS OF MARRIAGE.

YES! THE ANSWER, OF COURSE, IS 'I'.

SPOT the DIFFERENCE

It is not always easy to spot when someone is deceiving you. In this test can YOU tell who is telling the truth and who is lying?

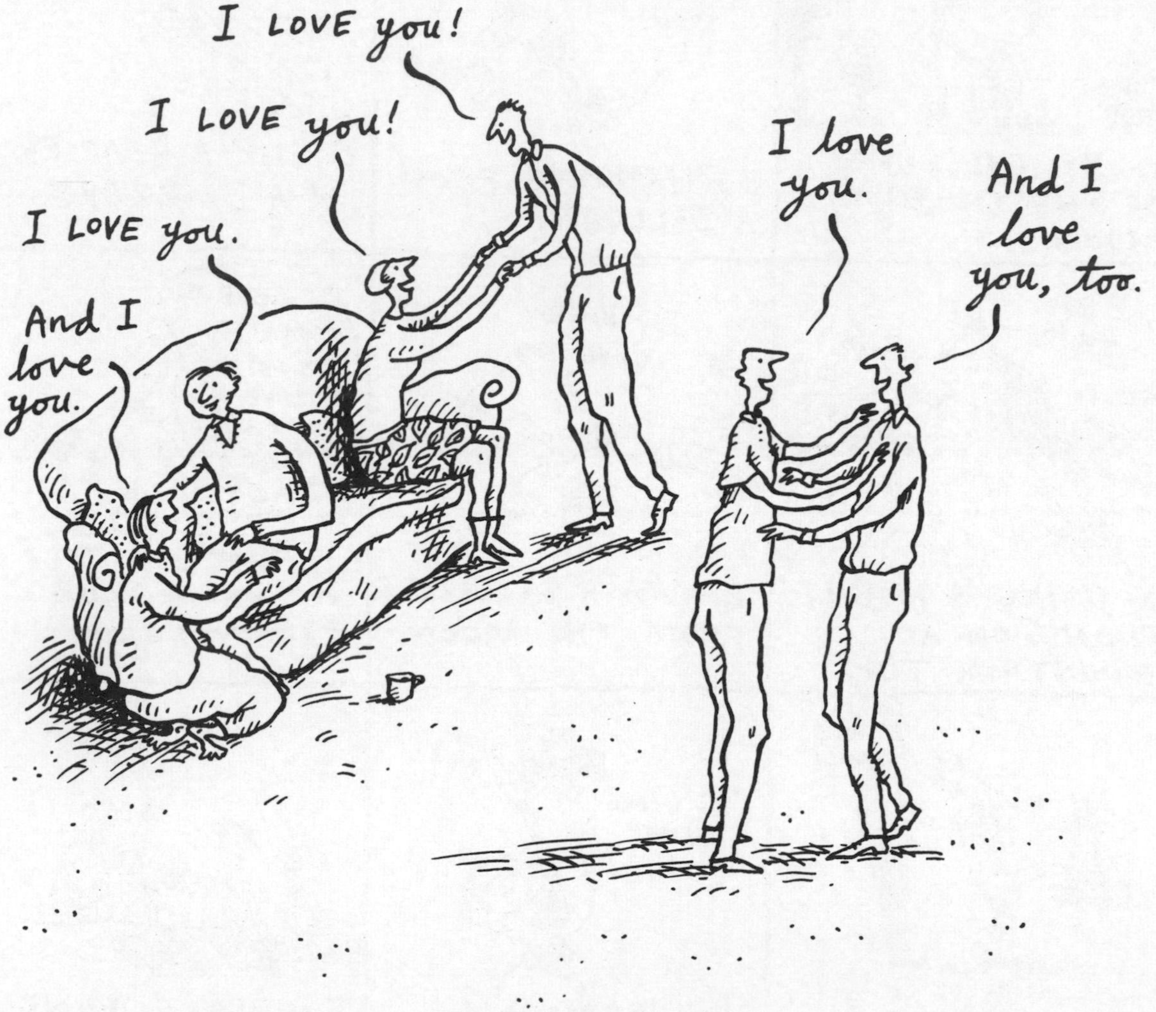

I LOVE you!
I LOVE you!
I LOVE you.
And I love you.
I love you.
And I love you, too.

(There is an ANSWER somewhere in this book. Can you find it?)

page 62

4

THE PRESSURES OF LOVE!

100%
100%

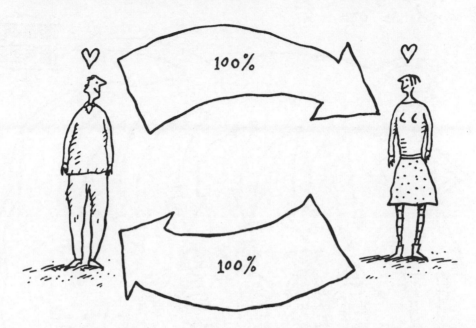

At the start of a relationship 100% of each person's love is directed towards their partner. Soon, however, it becomes divided and diluted. For example:

SELF
PARTNER
SPORT
DOG
PARTNER
SHOPPING
SELF
CAT

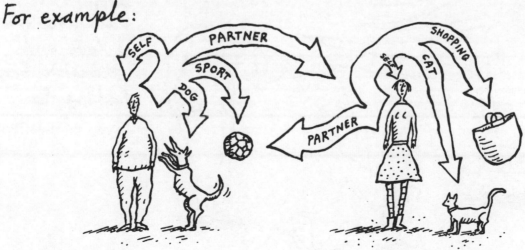

In no time at all LOVE is spread thinly between partner, children, job, friends, parents, home, car, pets and so on.

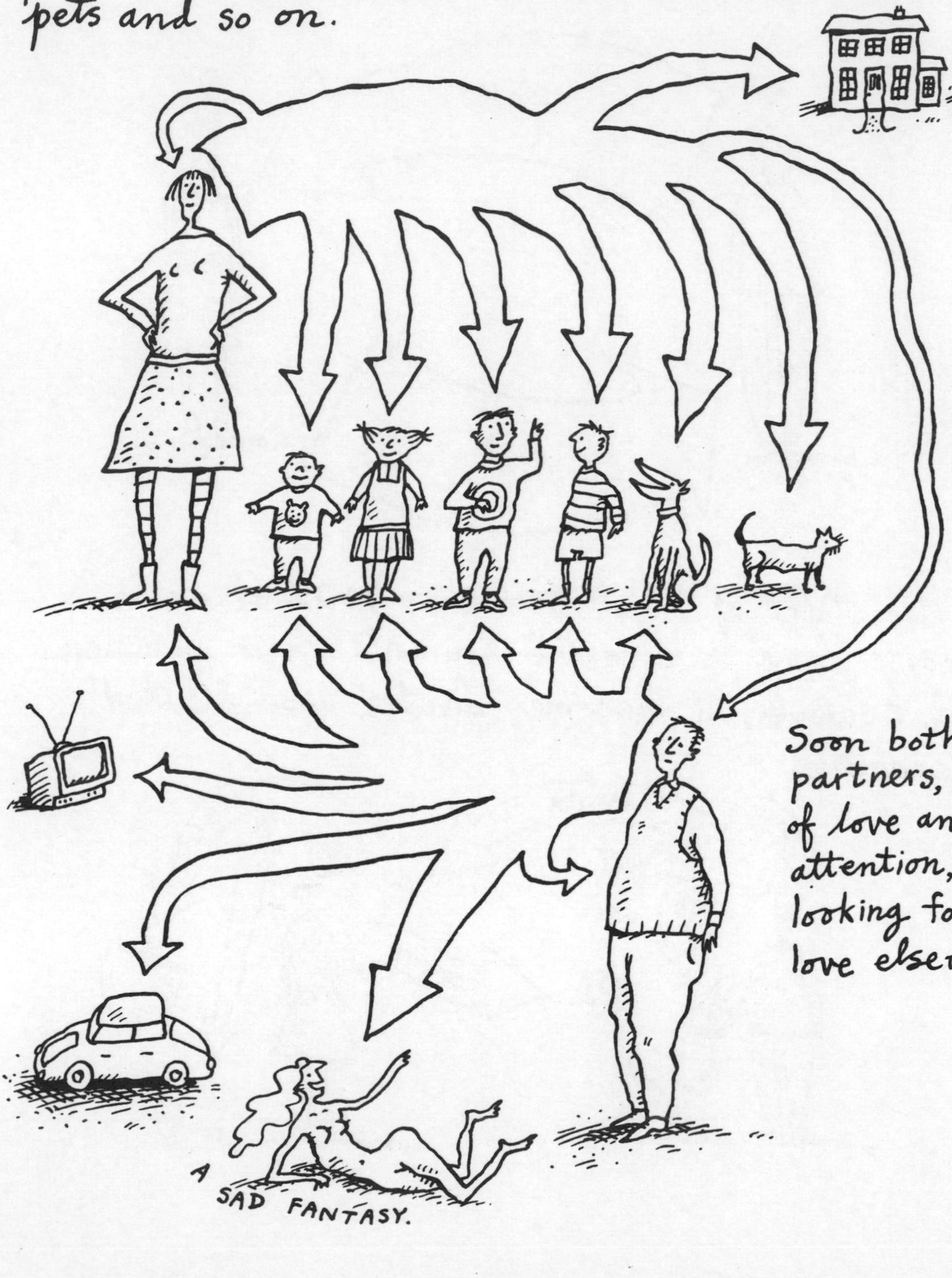
A SAD FANTASY.

Soon both partners, starved of love and attention, begin looking for love elsewhere...

A PIE-IN-THE-SKY GRAPH SHOWING A YOUNG PERSON'S HIGH EXPECTATIONS OF LOVE.

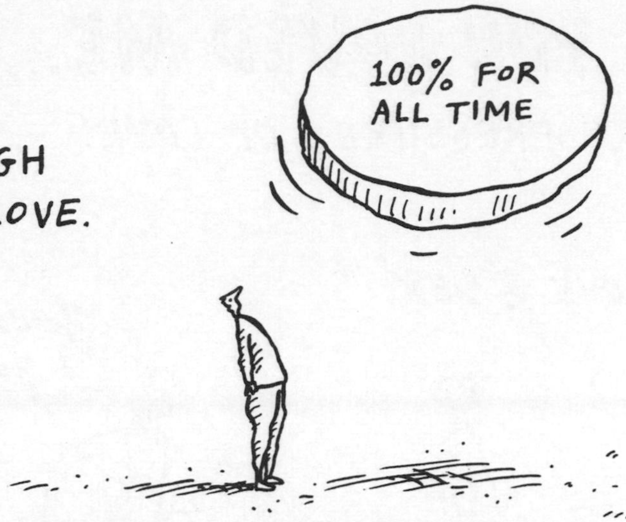
100% FOR ALL TIME

THIS PIE-DOWN-TO-EARTH GRAPH SHOWS A MORE REALISTIC OUTCOME.

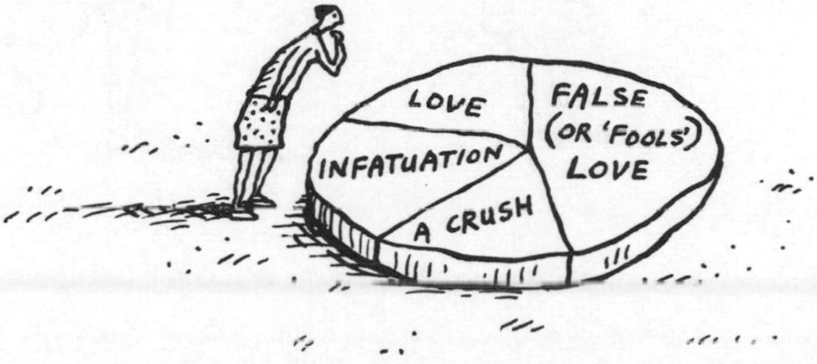
LOVE
FALSE (OR 'FOOLS') LOVE
INFATUATION
A CRUSH

THIS PIE GRAPH HAS CRASHED, KILLING AN INNOCENT BYSTANDER. ACCIDENT INVESTIGATORS WILL TRY TO PIECE IT BACK TOGETHER IN THE HOPE OF SOLVING ITS MYSTERIES.

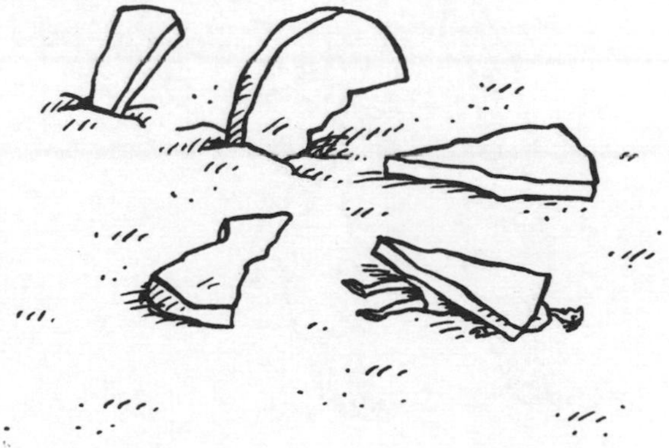

IF YOU LOVED ME...

MORE PRESSURES OF LOVE!

LOVE & SEX

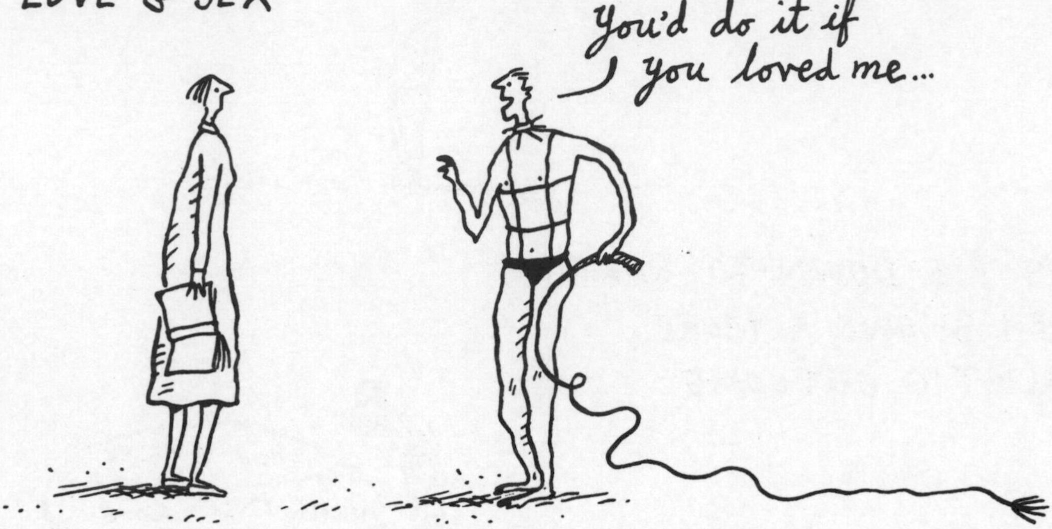
You'd do it if you loved me...

LOVE & KIDS

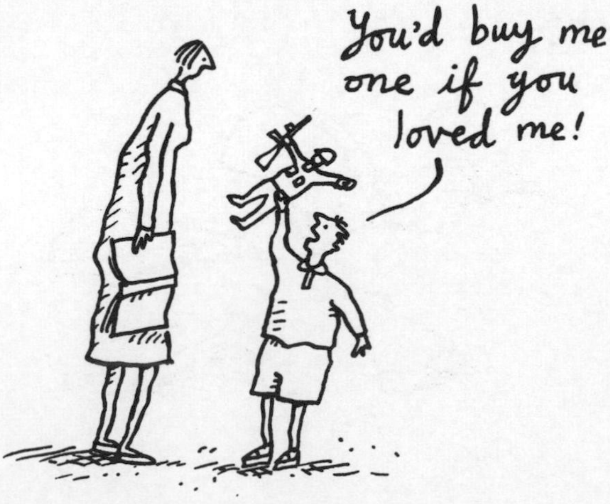
You'd buy me one if you loved me!

LOVE & A DOG

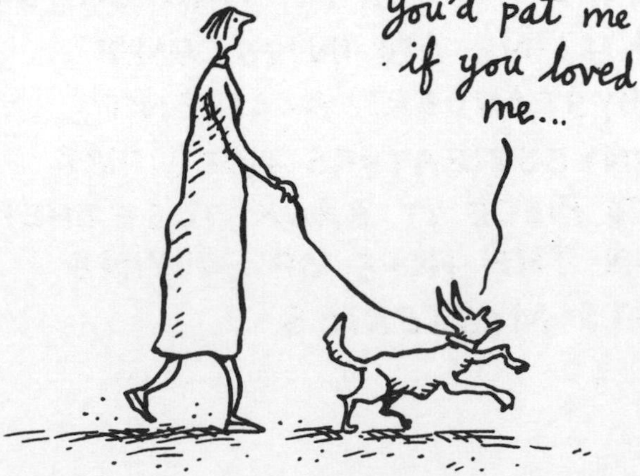
You'd pat me if you loved me...

LOVE & CHOCOLATE

You'd eat me if you loved me...
I'm dieting.

LOVE & DEATH

You'd unplug my life support machine if you loved me...

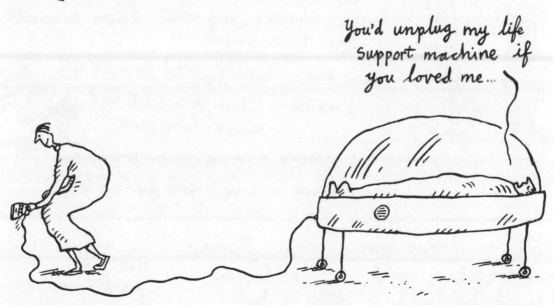

TESTING THE STRENGTH OF YOUR PARTNER'S LOVE

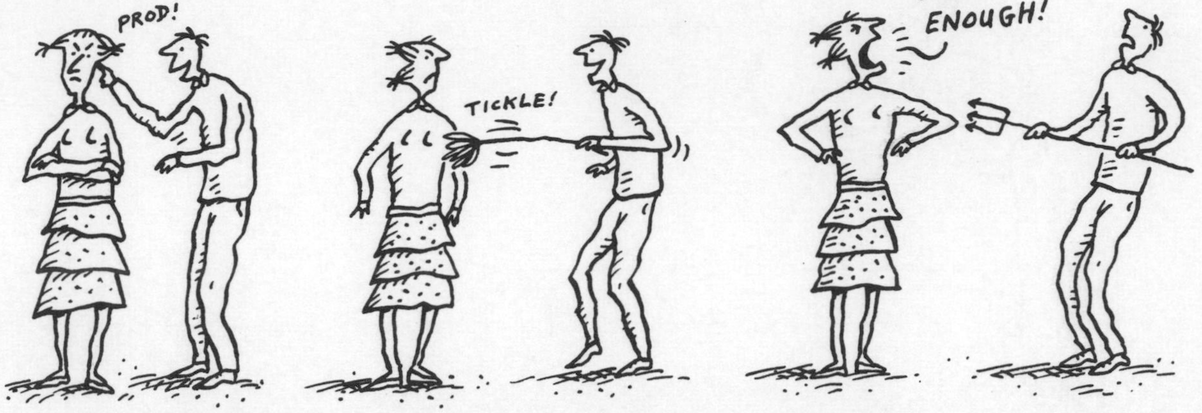
PROD!
TICKLE!
OKAY, THAT'S ENOUGH!

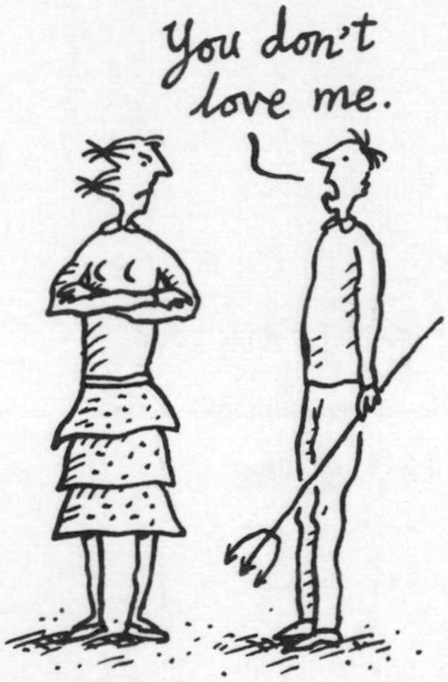
You don't love me.

OTHER METHODS:

HIM ~ Be as horrible, mean, grumpy, selfish and nasty as possible until she throws you out, then consult this time guide:

1 DAY - hardly loved you at all.

1 WEEK - liked you a bit but didn't love you.

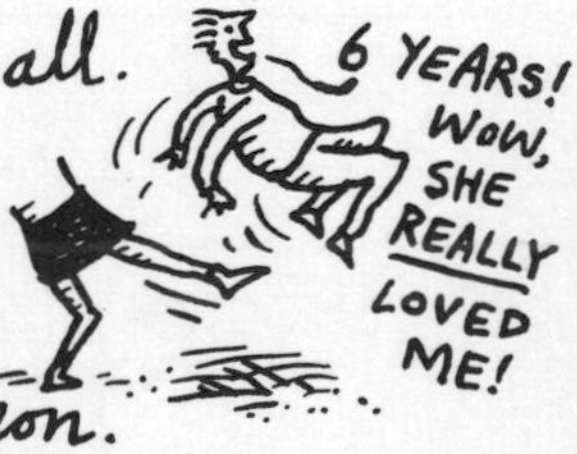
6 YEARS! WOW, SHE REALLY LOVED ME!

1 MONTH - loved you a smidgeon.

1 YEAR - loved you quite a lot.

HER ~ Offer him his freedom and see if he takes it.

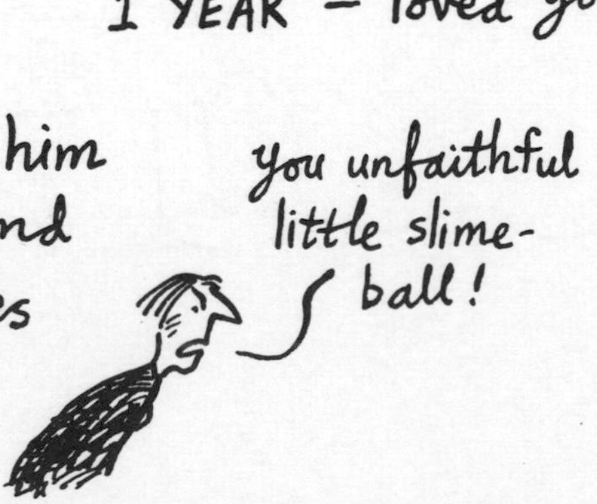
You unfaithful little slime-ball!

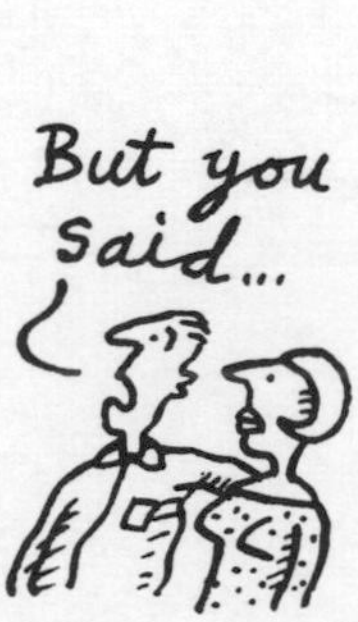
But you said...

ALTERNATIVELY

Give him some rope as a surprise gift.

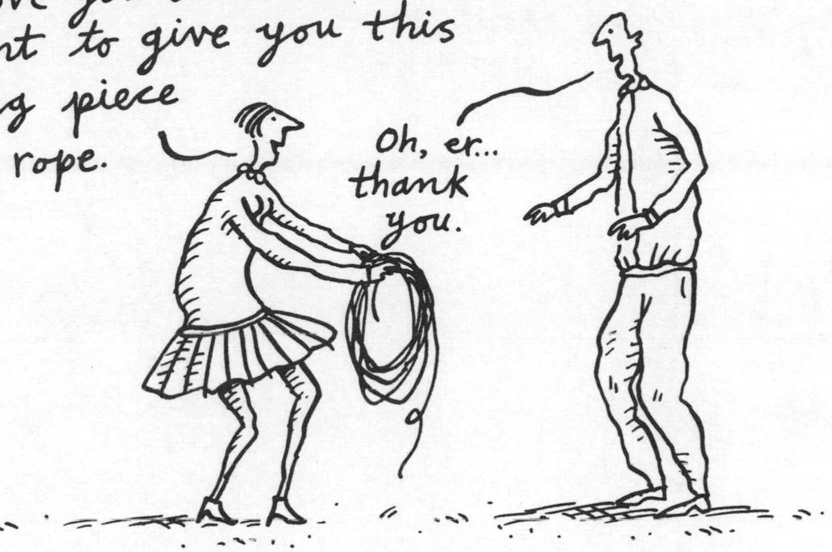

I love you so much I want to give you this long piece of rope.
Oh, er... thank you.

LATER...

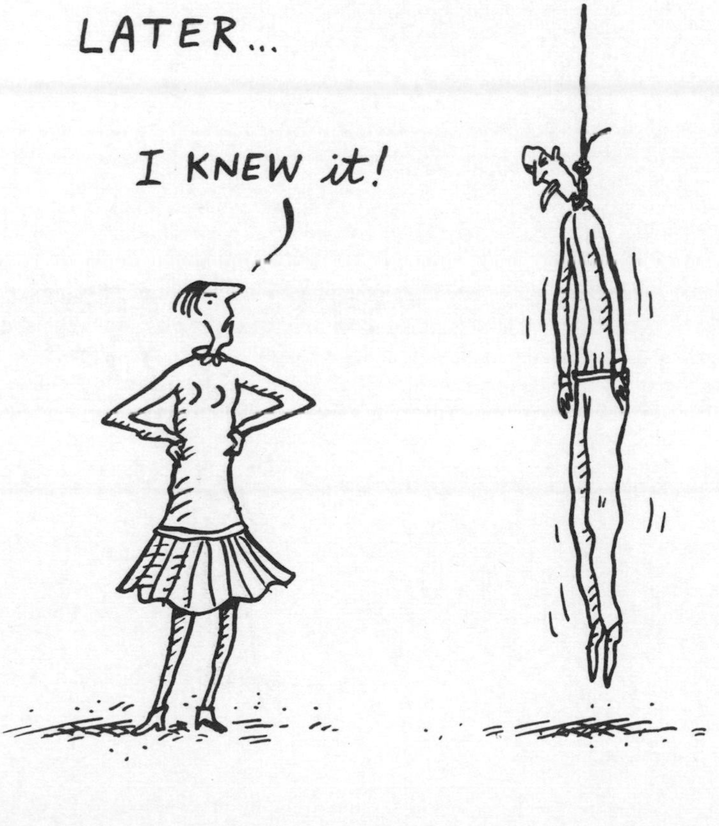

I KNEW it!

Can you TRUST your partner, or not? Here is

A USEFUL TEST FOR TRUST

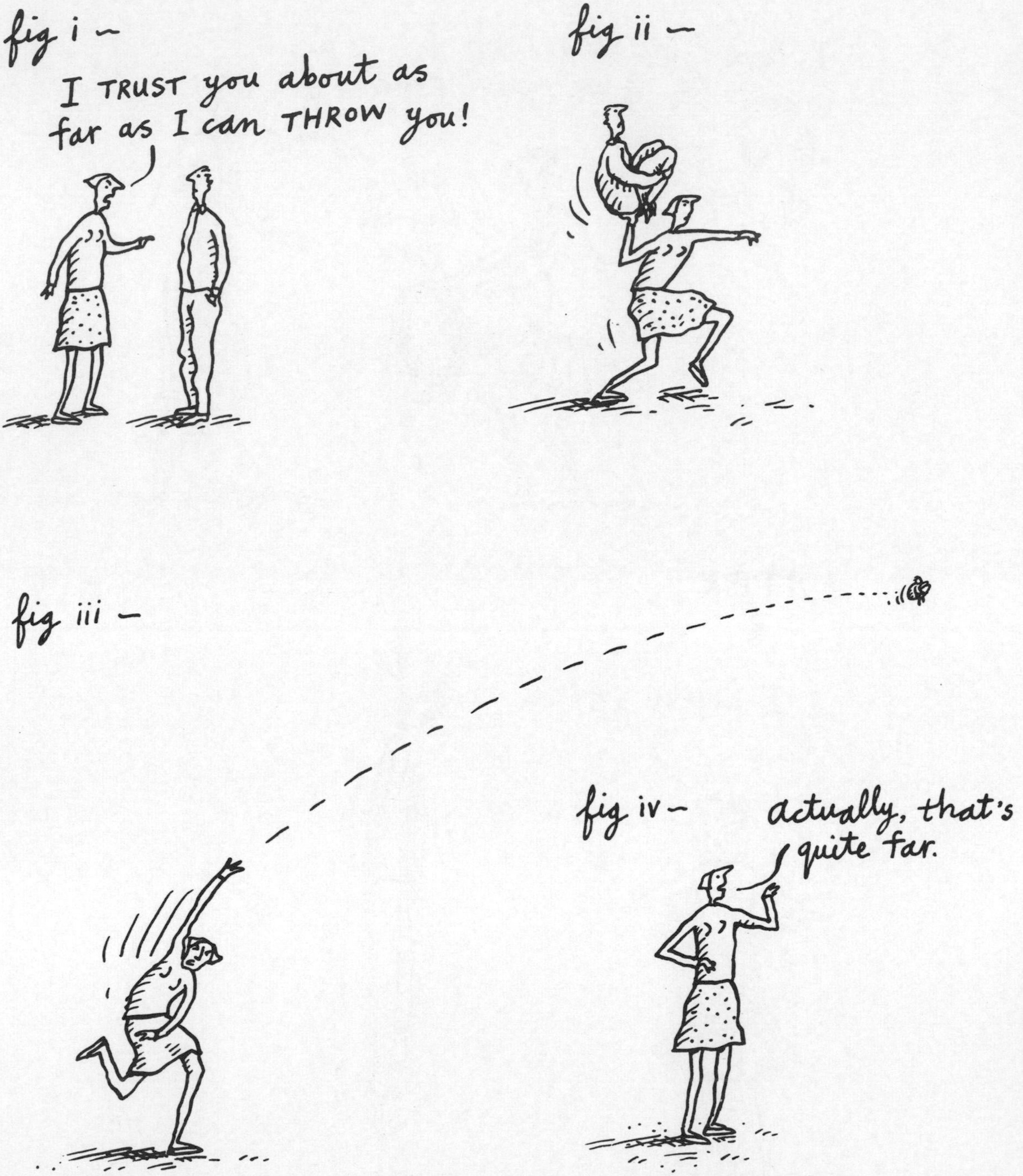

fig i –
I TRUST you about as far as I can THROW you!
fig ii –
fig iii –
fig iv –
actually, that's quite far.

But of course,

LOVE MEANS FORGIVING...

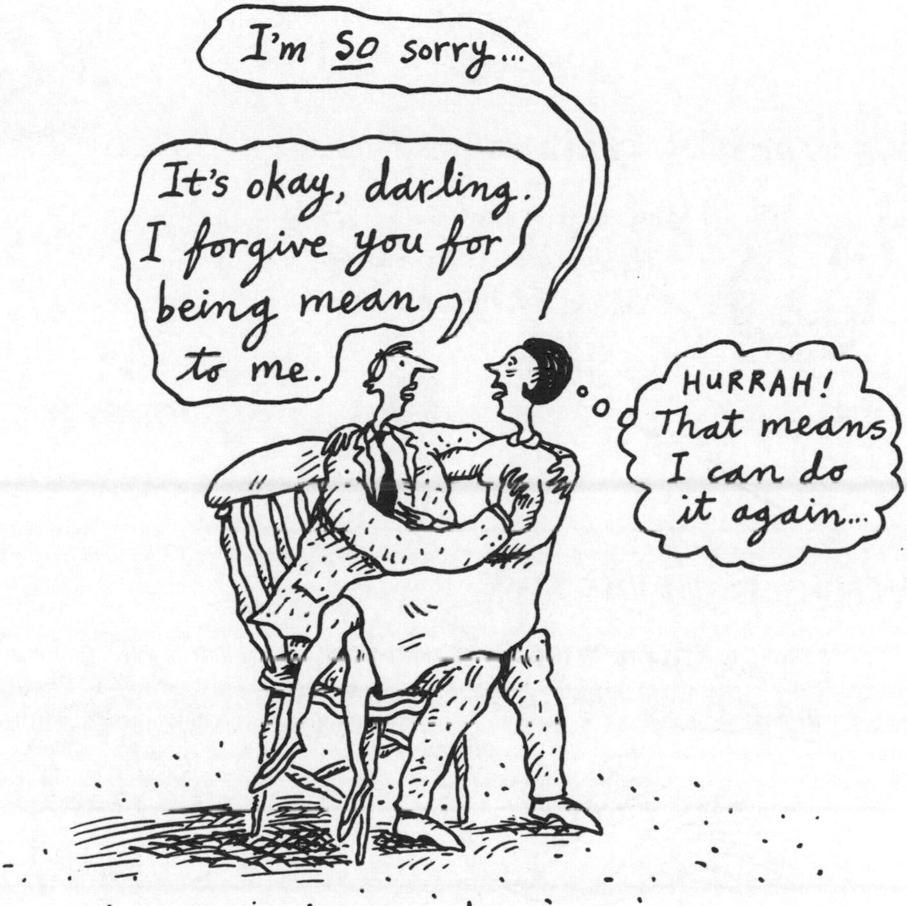
I'm SO sorry...
It's okay, darling. I forgive you for being mean to me.
HURRAH! That means I can do it again...

SOME MYTHS ABOUT LOVE

i – CUPID CAUSES PEOPLE TO FALL IN LOVE.

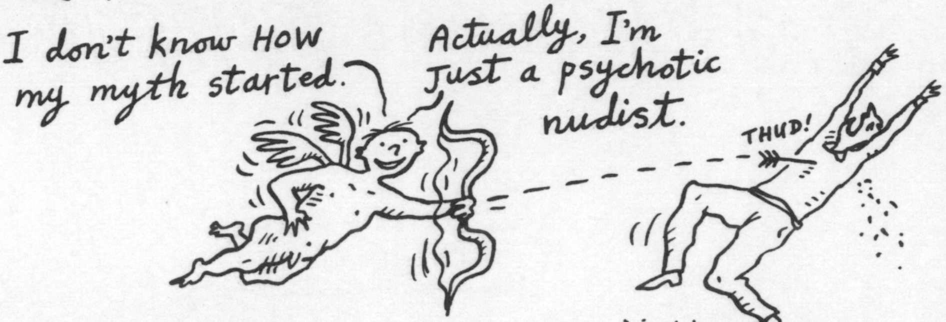
I don't know HOW my myth started.
Actually, I'm Just a psychotic nudist.
THUD!

ii – THE MOON IS ROMANTIC.

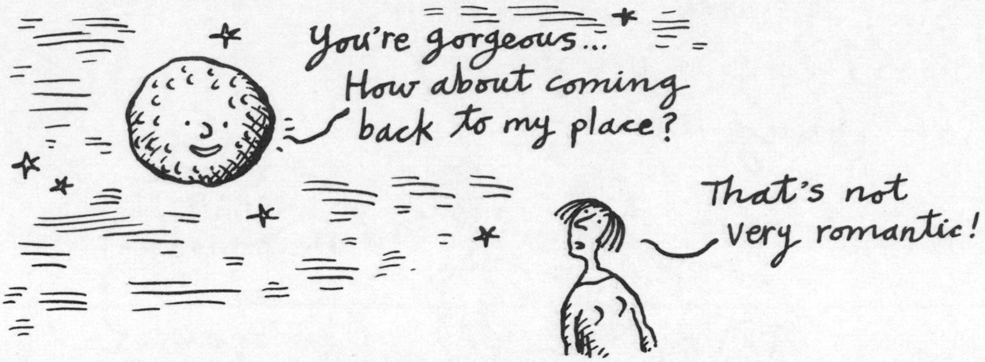
You're gorgeous... How about coming back to my place?
That's not very romantic!

iii – VENUS IS SEDUCTIVE.

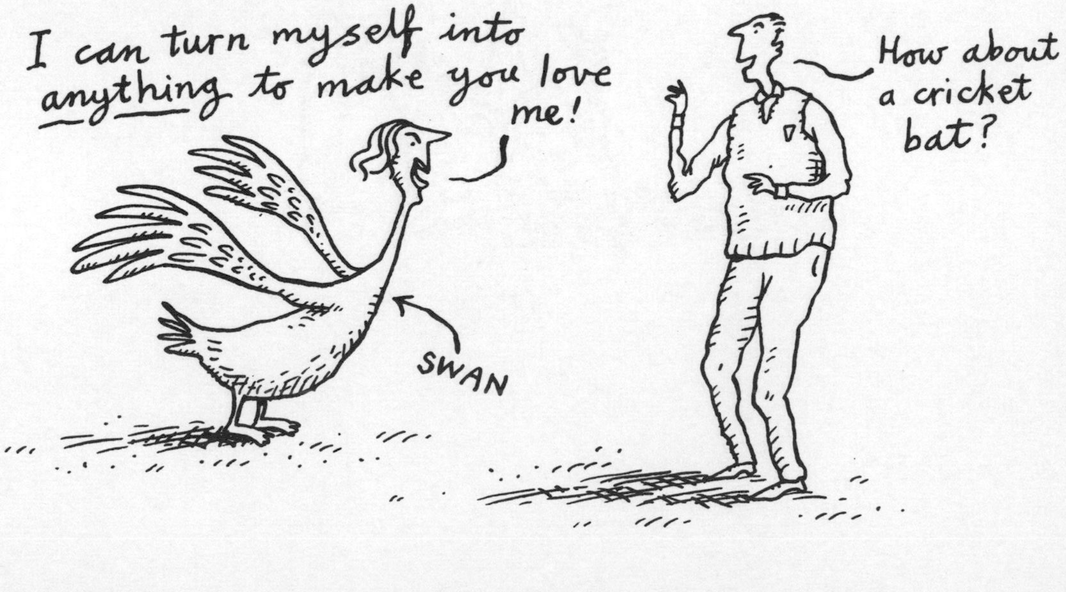
I can turn myself into anything to make you love me!
How about a cricket bat?
SWAN

SACRIFICING A HUSBAND to VENUS the GODDESS OF LOVE

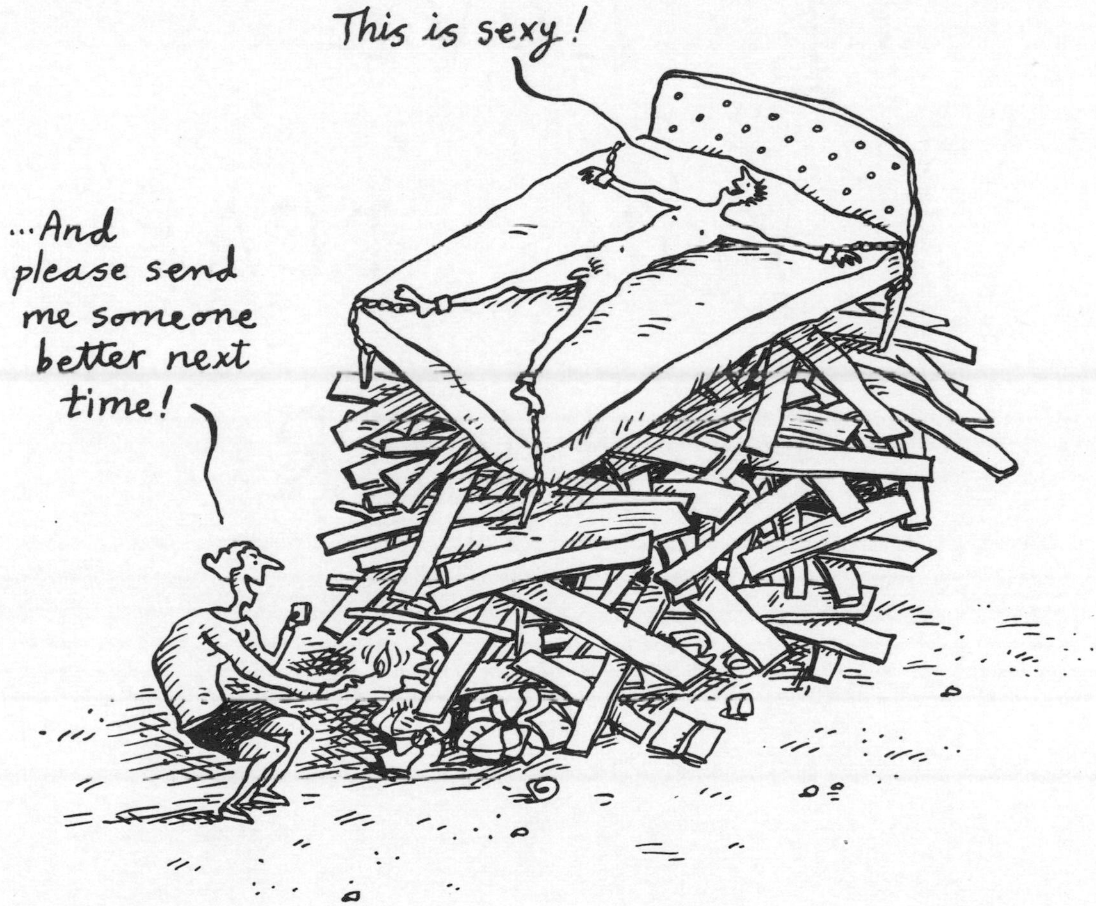
This is sexy!
...And please send me someone better next time!

AN <u>AFFIRMATIVE</u> PAGE

In case your spirits are a little low following the true-life revelations in this book, I'd like to take this opportunity to say, sincerely,

I LOVE YOU, DEAR READER.

Now, read on...

9 USEFUL TRIED & TESTED WAYS TO SHOW SOMEONE THAT YOU LOVE THEM

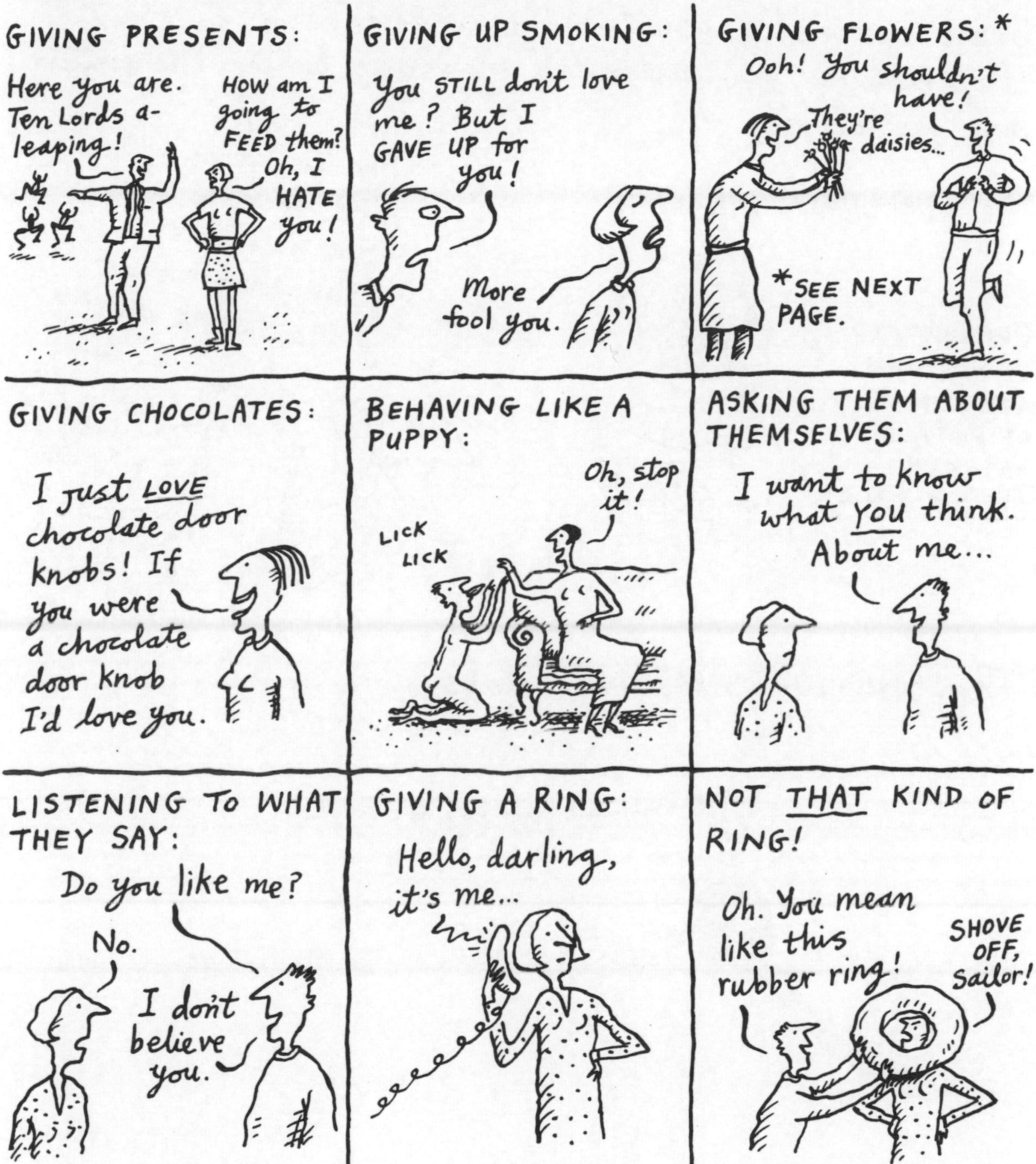

GIVING PRESENTS:
Here you are. Ten Lords a-leaping!
HOW am I going to FEED them?
Oh, I HATE you!
GIVING UP SMOKING:
You STILL don't love me? But I GAVE UP for you!
More fool you.
GIVING FLOWERS: *
Ooh! You shouldn't have!
They're daisies...
*SEE NEXT PAGE.
GIVING CHOCOLATES:
I just LOVE chocolate door knobs! If you were a chocolate door knob I'd love you.
BEHAVING LIKE A PUPPY:
LICK
LICK
Oh, stop it!
ASKING THEM ABOUT THEMSELVES:
I want to know what YOU think. About me...
LISTENING TO WHAT THEY SAY:
Do you like me?
No.
I don't believe you.
GIVING A RING:
Hello, darling, it's me...
NOT THAT KIND OF RING!
Oh. You mean like this rubber ring!
SHOVE OFF, Sailor!

SAY IT WITH FLOWERS

These versions of the traditional floral gift have been specially genetically engineered so that they deliver the intended message when the petals are pulled off.

The SHE-LOVES-ME rose:

GUARANTEED TO HAVE AN ODD NUMBER OF PETALS OR YOUR MONEY BACK!

She loves me...
She loves me not...
She loves me...
She loves me not...
She LOVES ME!!

You were supposed to put it in a vase of water.

The SHE-LOVES-ME-NOT daisy

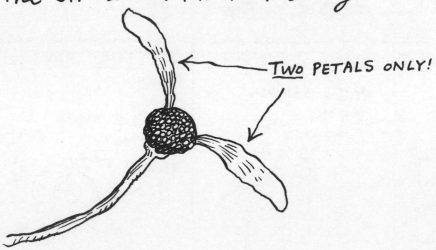

TWO PETALS ONLY!

My floral memento ~

Instructions:

USE THIS PAGE TO PRESERVE A FLOWER GIVEN TO YOU BY YOUR LOVED ONE (OR TWO, OR THREE). TAPE THE BLOOM TO THE PAGE, CLOSE THE BOOK AND PRESS IT UNDER YOUR MATTRESS. HAVING FREQUENT, PASSIONATE SEX **ON** THE MATTRESS WILL SPEED THE PROCESS ALONG.

5

WAXING & WANING

Here is a scientific version of the SHE-LOVES-ME rose on page 76. To find out if YOU are <u>IN</u> or <u>OUT</u> of love, simply close your eyes, turn the book around twice then plonk your finger onto the diagram below.

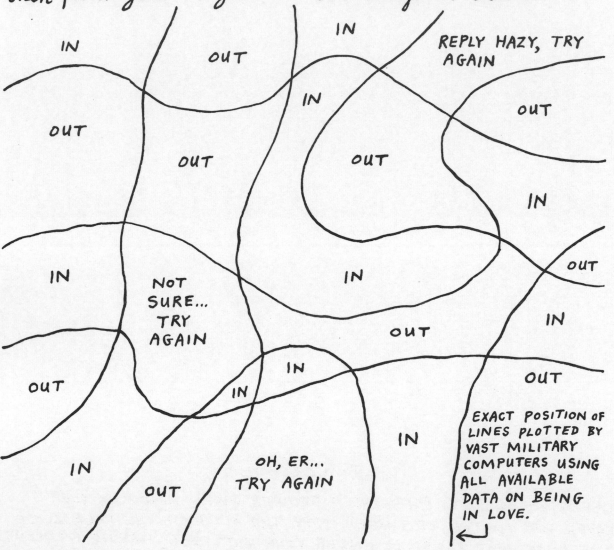

IN

OUT

IN

REPLY HAZY, TRY AGAIN

IN

OUT

OUT

OUT

OUT

IN

IN

IN

OUT

NOT SURE... TRY AGAIN

IN

OUT

IN

OUT

OUT

IN

IN

IN

OH, ER... TRY AGAIN

IN

EXACT POSITION OF LINES PLOTTED BY VAST MILITARY COMPUTERS USING ALL AVAILABLE DATA ON BEING IN LOVE.

THE PHASES OF LOVE

It is, of course, unusual for love to continue at the same pitch month after month and year after year. Usually it goes through various phases. Here are a few.

BEGINNING:

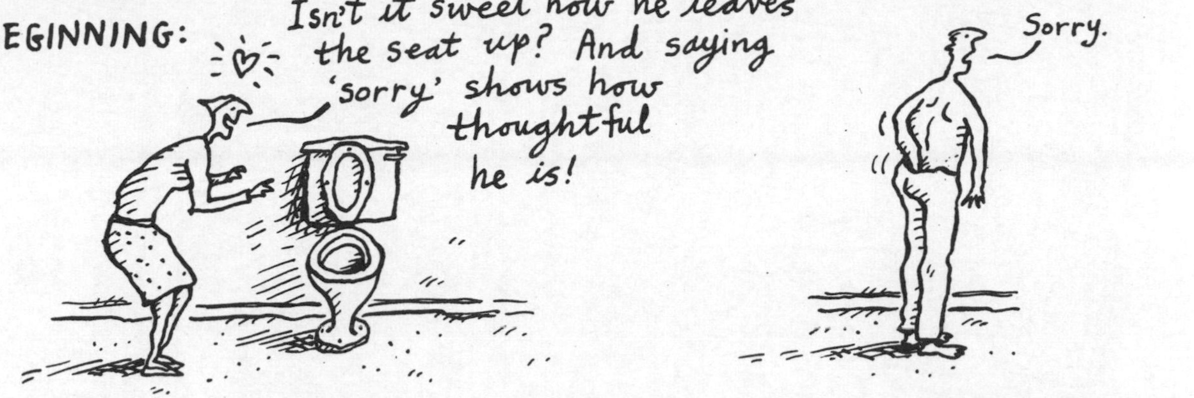
Isn't it sweet how he leaves the seat up? And saying 'sorry' shows how thoughtful he is!
Sorry.

MIDDLE:

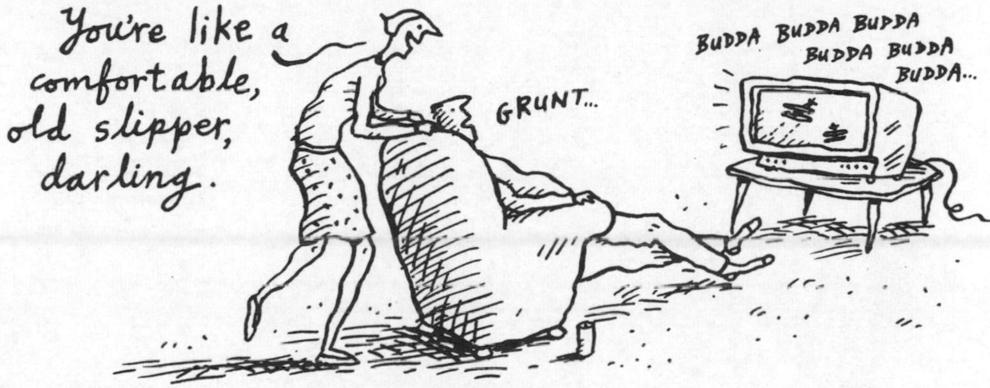
You're like a comfortable, old slipper, darling.
GRUNT...
BUDDA BUDDA BUDDA BUDDA BUDDA BUDDA...

BEGINNING OF THE END:

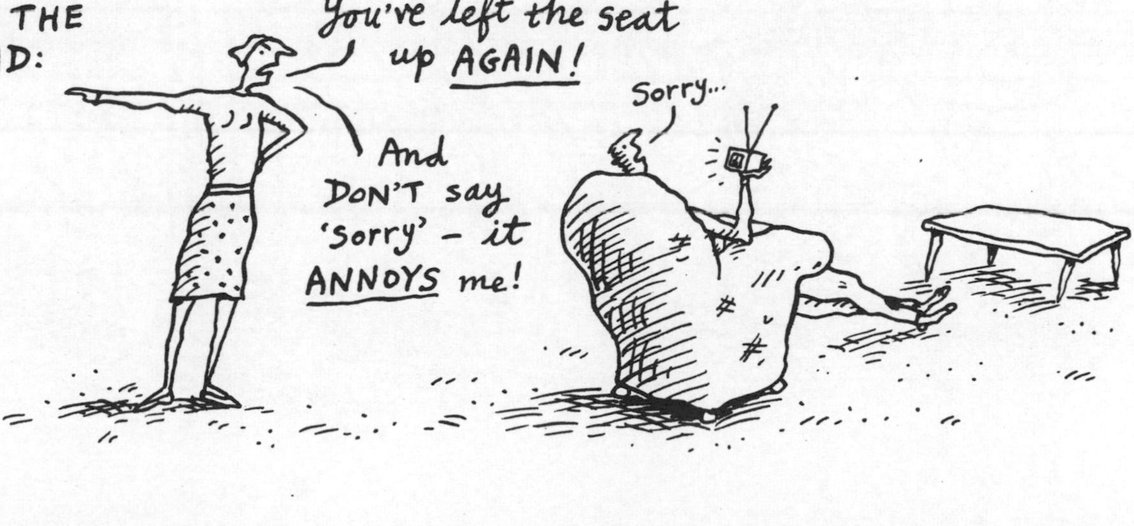
You've left the seat up AGAIN!
And DON'T say 'sorry' – it ANNOYS me!
Sorry...

How LOVE gets buried under REAL LIFE...

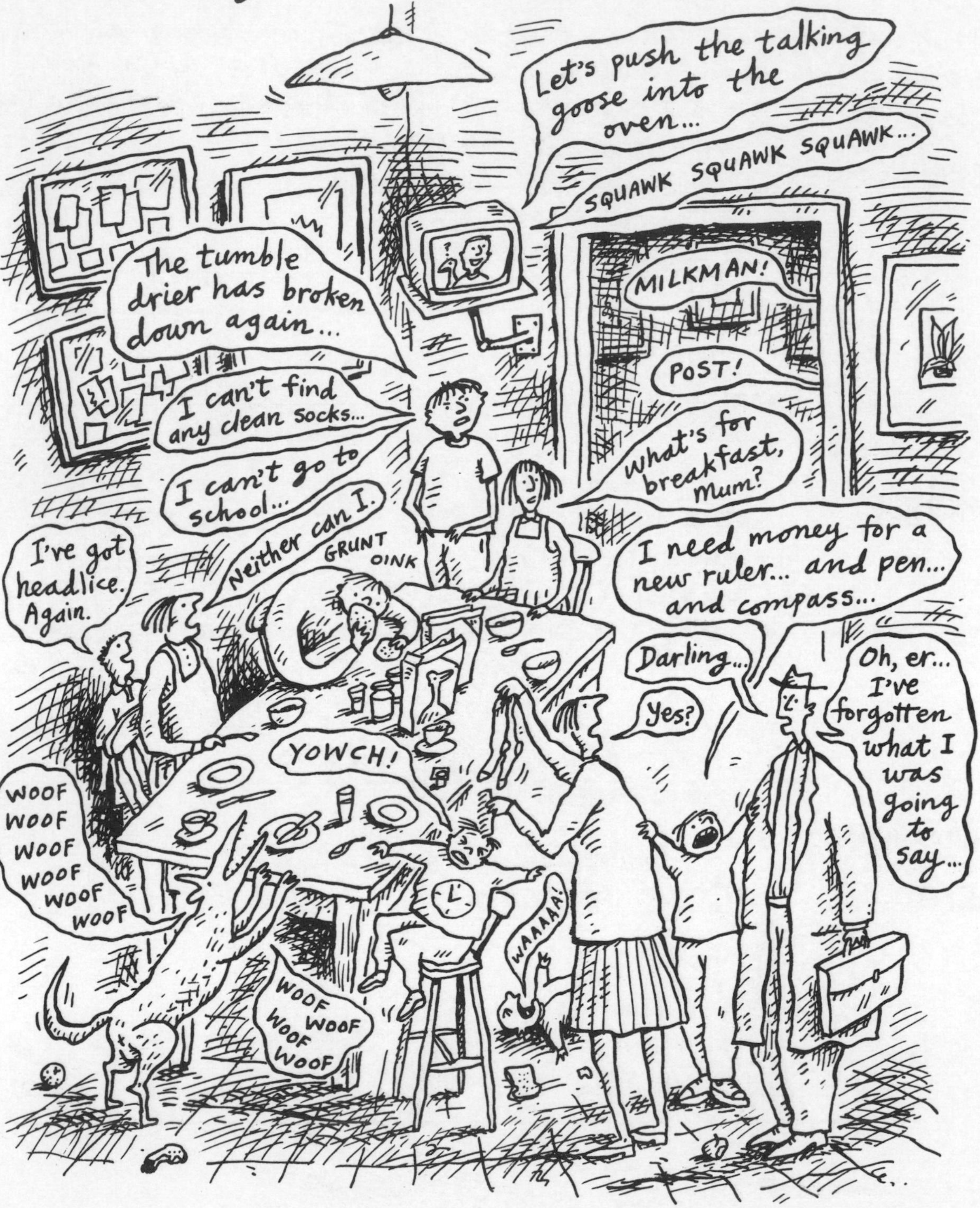

Let's push the talking goose into the oven...
SQUAWK SQUAWK SQUAWK...
The tumble drier has broken down again...
MILKMAN!
POST!
I can't find any clean socks...
what's for breakfast, Mum?
I can't go to school...
Neither can I.
GRUNT
OINK
I've got headlice. Again.
I need money for a new ruler... and pen... and compass...
Darling...
Yes?
Oh, er... I've forgotten what I was going to say...
YOWCH!
WOOF WOOF WOOF WOOF WOOF WOOF
WAAAAA!
WOOF WOOF WOOF WOOF

TRYING to RE-IGNITE that OLD FLAME of PASSION!

HOW ABOUT SOME EXPERIMENTAL SEX?

MEN don't think with their minds (see fig 1) so usually the direct approach works well.

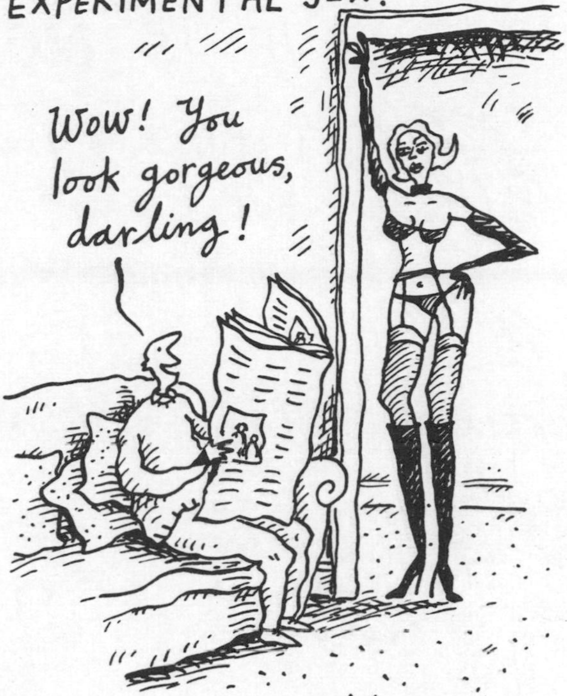
Wow! You look gorgeous, darling!

fig 1 - HOW MEN THINK:

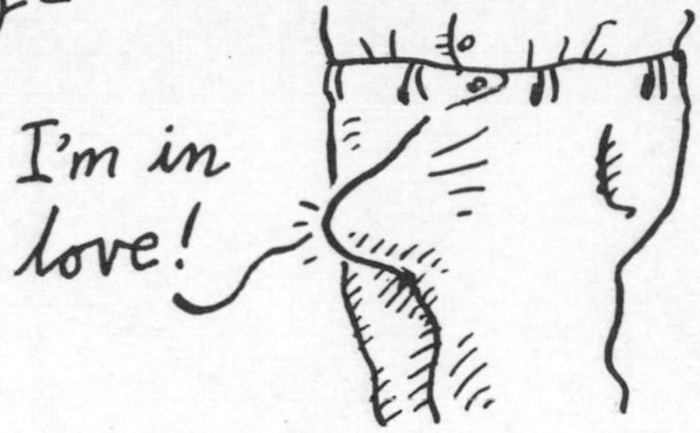
I'm in love!

WOMEN, on the other hand, are more romantic so the direct approach usually backfires.

Try growing your chest hair, buying a frock coat and rescuing her from the supermarket queue on a white stallion.

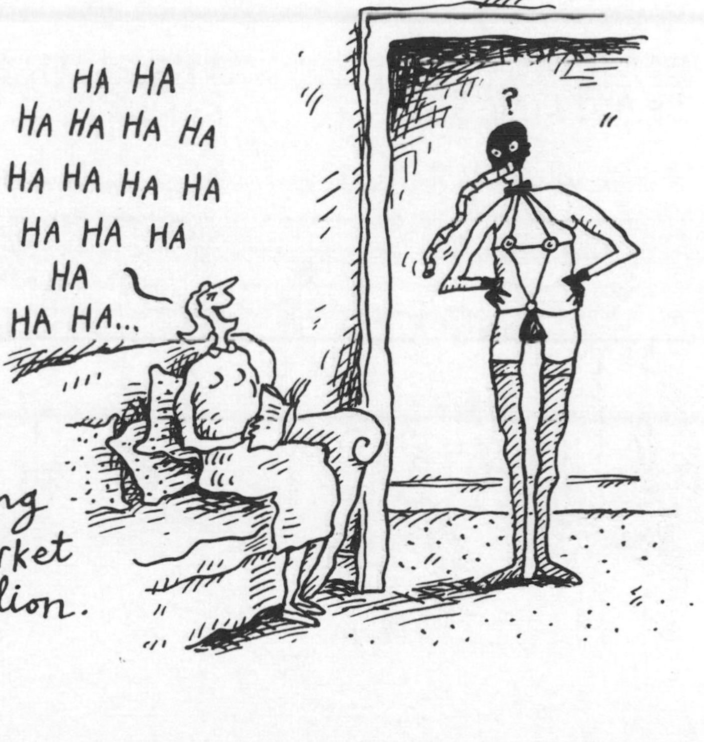
HA HA
HA HA HA HA
HA HA HA HA
HA HA HA
HA
HA HA...
?

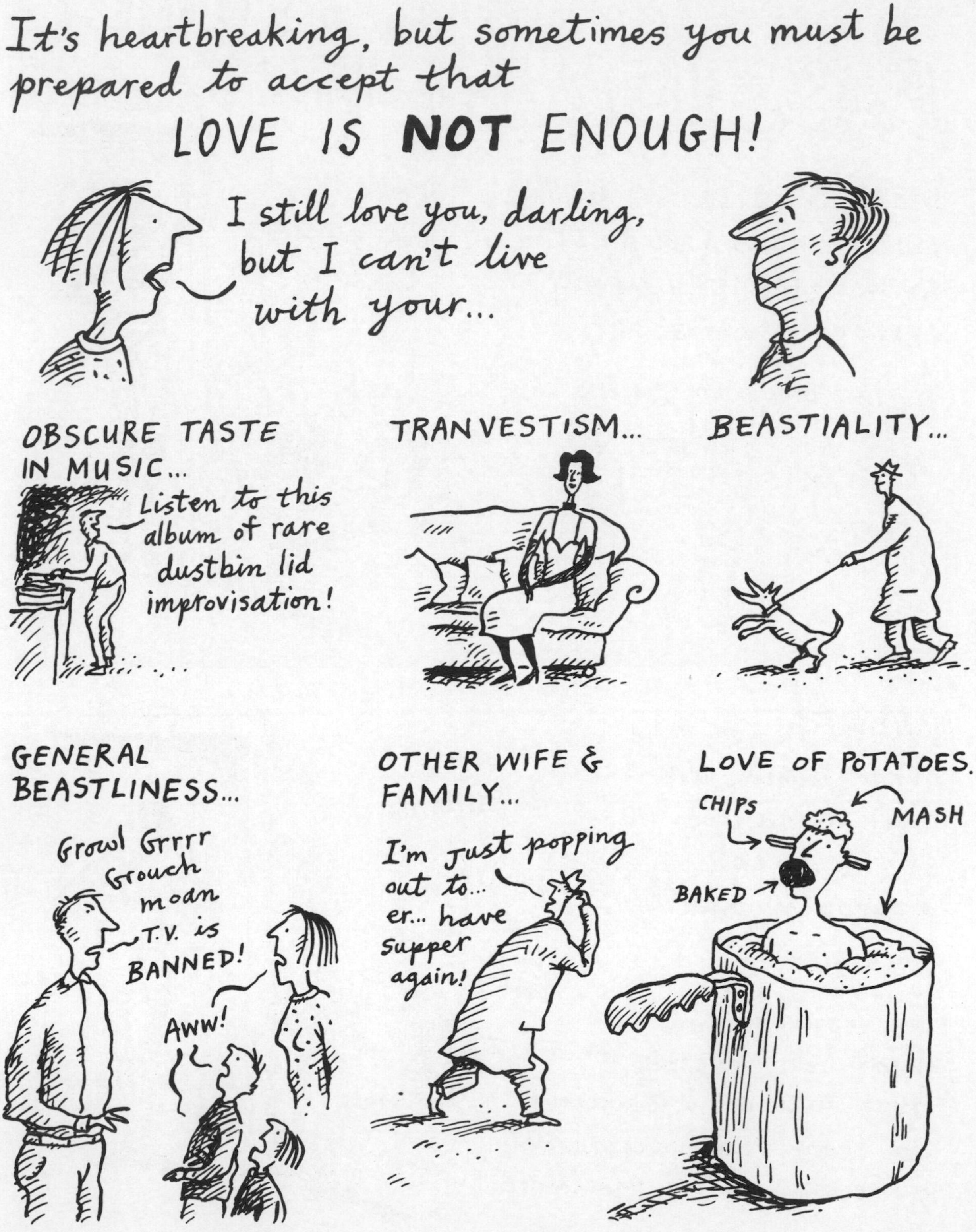
It's heartbreaking, but sometimes you must be prepared to accept that
LOVE IS NOT ENOUGH!
I still love you, darling, but I can't live with your...
OBSCURE TASTE IN MUSIC...
Listen to this album of rare dustbin lid improvisation!
TRANVESTISM...
BEASTIALITY...
GENERAL BEASTLINESS...
Growl Grrrr Grouch moan T.V. is BANNED!
AWW!
OTHER WIFE & FAMILY...
I'm just popping out to... er... have supper again!
LOVE OF POTATOES.
CHIPS
MASH
BAKED

So, when LOVE fails to CONQUER ALL and you have to END YOUR AFFAIR, here are some possible ways you might react...

BLANKLY:

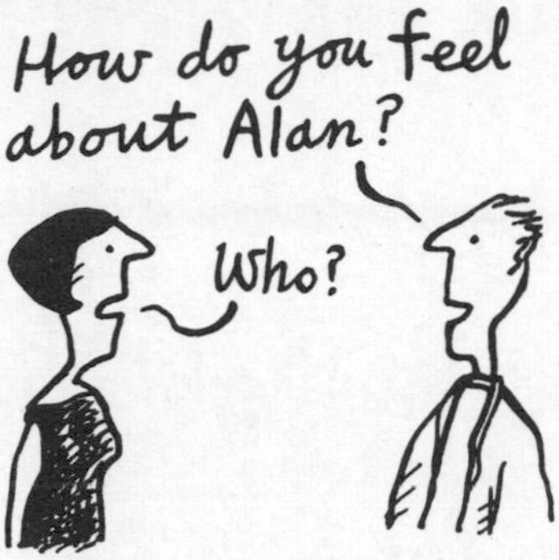
How do you feel about Alan?
Who?

PRACTICALLY:

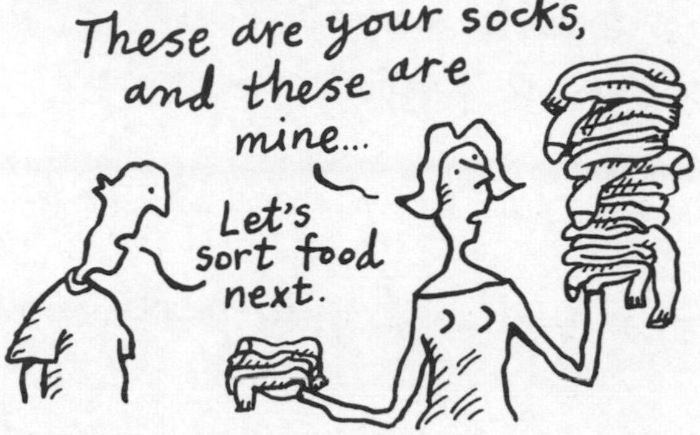
These are your socks, and these are mine...
Let's sort food next.

REGRESSIVELY:

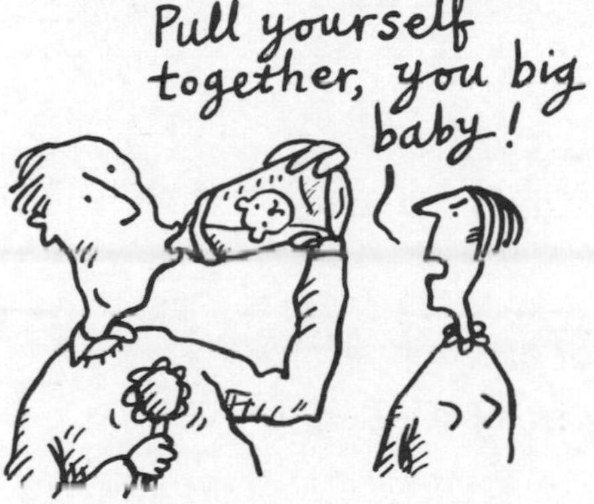
Pull yourself together, you big baby!

AQUATICALLY:

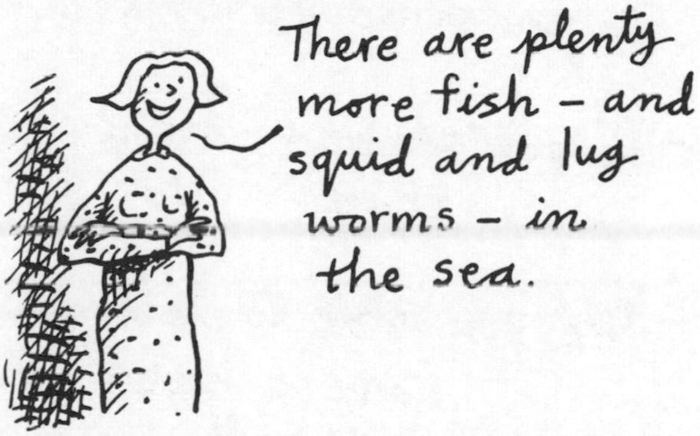
There are plenty more fish - and squid and lug worms - in the sea.

ACTIVELY:

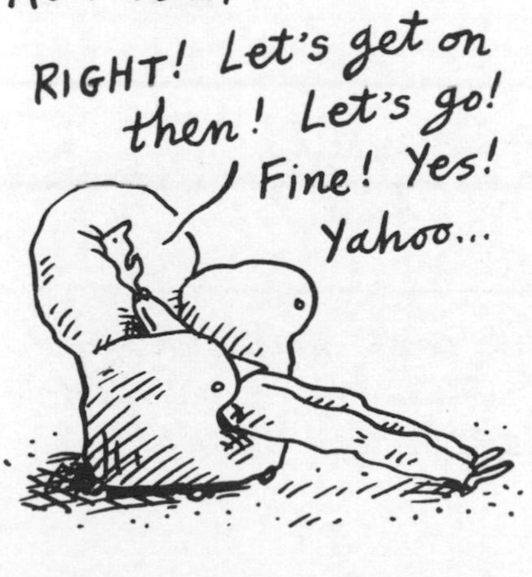
RIGHT! Let's get on then! Let's go! Fine! Yes! Yahoo...

CLINGINGLY:

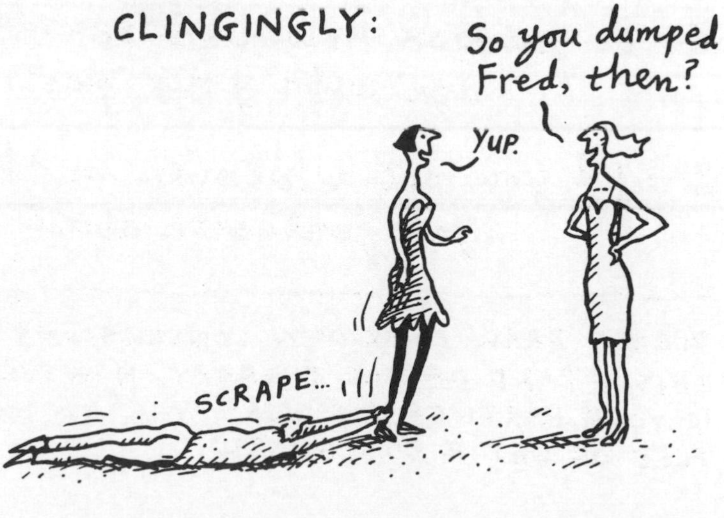
So you dumped Fred, then?
YUP.
SCRAPE...

THE TRUTH ABOUT LOVE

Now that you are nearly at the end of this book, perhaps it is time to grit your teeth and learn the truth about YOURSELF and YOUR PARTNER! Here is a short test:

	YES	NO

1 - Do you keep secrets from your partner? ☐ ☐

2 - Do you and your partner make each other laugh? ☐ ☐

3 - Do you imagine someone else during sex? ☐ ☐

4 - Do you stay at work as long as possible? ☐ ☐

5 - Do you phone up for no good reason other than to hear your partner's voice? ☐ ☐

6 - Are you able to tell your partner if they have a habit which annoys you? ☐ ☐

7 - Do you look forward to spending your old age with your partner? ☐ ☐

8 - If you met a hitman in the pub would you fantasise about hiring him? ☐ ☐

PLEASE DRAW YOUR OWN CONCLUSIONS FROM YOUR ANSWERS - THIS IS PART OF THE THERAPY. HOWEVER, I WILL POINT OUT THAT IF YOUR PARTNER ANSWERS 'YES' TO NUMBER 8, YOU SHOULD FLEE OR GET A BODYGUARD.

PERHAPS the problem is that you are INCAPABLE of FALLING IN LOVE! But don't worry – yet. To find out for sure one way or the other

ASK THE LOVE CONSULTANT.

Printed in EMOTIONALLY REACTIVE INK, the LOVE CONSULTANT changes colour according to the emotional polarity of your body!

SIMPLY place your hand on the LOVE CONSULTANT for about a minute and the box relevant to you will turn a deep red.

SORRY- LOVE IS **NOT** POSSIBLE FOR YOU	HURRAH! YOU **CAN** FALL IN LOVE	YOU ARE ABLE TO LOVE YOURSELF BUT NOT OTHERS
GO BACK ONE SPACE	YOU CAN FEEL **LUST** BUT NOT LOVE	GO AND HAVE A COLD SHOWER

TROUBLE-SHOOTING:

If the LOVE CONSULTANT does not appear to be working, please consider the following possibilities:

i – Your emotional needs are off the LOVE CONSULTANT'S scale.

ii – You inadvertently bought the NON-INTERACTIVE Mk 1 edition of this book – check serial number on page 6.

iii – You are dead.

THE LENGTH OF A PIECE OF STRING*

If you're finding love elusive, why not let this SPECIAL OFFER take advantage of you? FILL IN the form below and post it to me, c/o my publishers, enclosing a SMALL ☐ MEDIUM ☐ LARGE ☑ donation.

Steven Appleby's PHILANTHROPIC & UTTERLY CONFIDENTIAL† DATING AGENCY

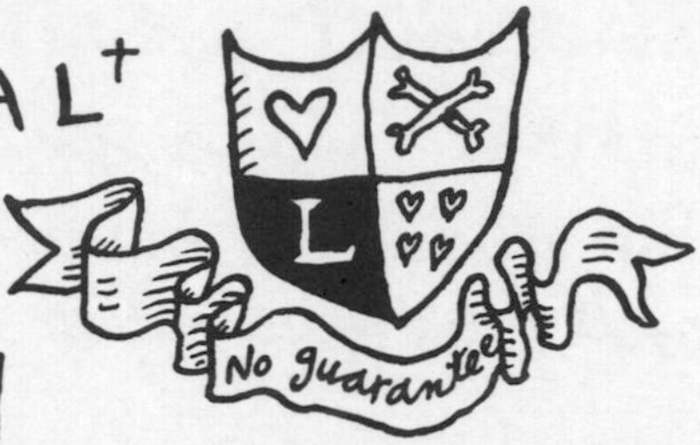
L
No guarantee

NAME ☐

AGE ☐

ADDRESS ☐

SEX ☐

I am looking for a MALE ☐ FEMALE ☐ WHATEVER ☐**

**Tick box or boxes according to your desires, urges or level of greed.

USE THIS SPACE TO WRITE ABOUT YOURSELF. ⇩

PLEASE ENCLOSE naked photos of yourself, friends, etc.

USE THIS SPACE TO DESCRIBE YOUR IDEAL MATE. ⇩

SIZE OF BODY PARTS

*USE STRING MENTIONED ABOVE TO ESTIMATE SIZE OF IDEAL BITS WANTED.

†'UTTERLY CONFIDENTIAL' is only the name of the agency. All submissions will be used in future books and cartoons.

DON'T FORGET TO SEND CHEQUE ☐ CASH ☑

INTO THE SUNSET...

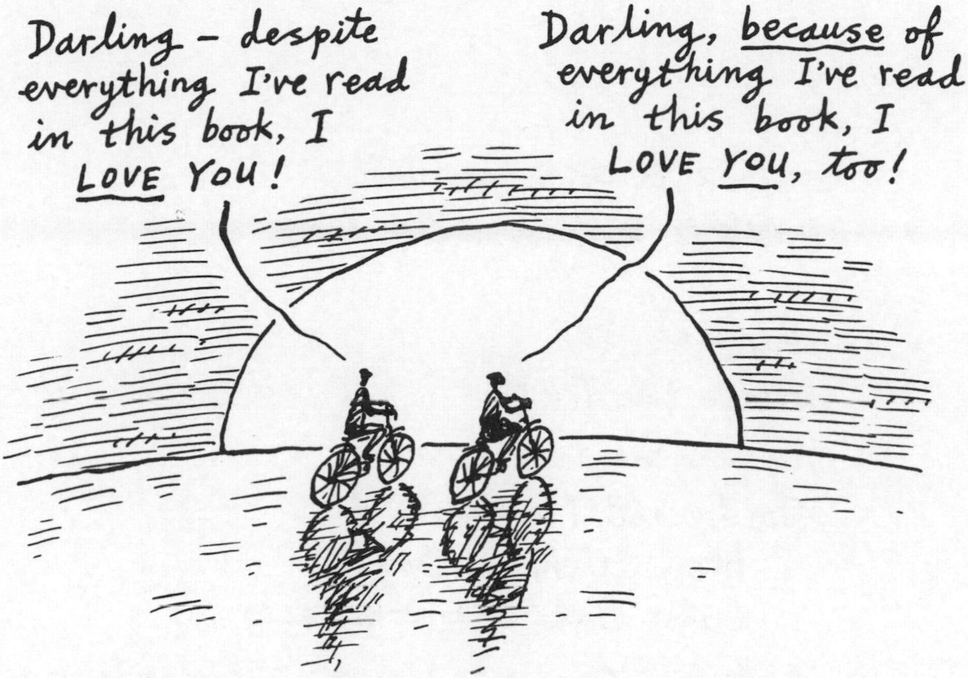

Darling – despite everything I've read in this book, I LOVE YOU!
Darling, because of everything I've read in this book, I LOVE YOU, too!

THANK GOODNESS for a HAPPY ENDING!
But please remember – the sun is 100 times more likely to damage your eyesight than masturbation, so when riding into the sunset ALWAYS wear dark, protective glasses or you'll go blind.

OTHER BOOKS you will
LOVE by Steven Appleby:

Normal Sex
Men - the Truth
Miserable Families
The Secret Thoughts of...
    Men; Women; Dogs;
    Cats; Babies & YOURSELF!

Antmen Carry Away My Thoughts
    As Soon As I Think Them
ALIEN INVASION! The Complete
    Guide To Having Children